LETTERS FROM AMERICA 1853 - 1860

LETTERS FROM AMERICA

1853 - 1860

Compiled and Edited by
T. Barry Davies

Published in 1991 by
The Self Publishing Association Ltd
Lloyds Bank Chambers
Upton-upon-Severn, Worcs
A MEMBER OF

in conjunction with
T. BARRY DAVIES

British Library Cataloguing in Publication Data
Letters from America 1853-1860.
    1. United States, history
    I. Davies, T. Barry
    973

ISBN 1 85421 127 7

Designed and produced by The Self Publishing Association Ltd.
Printed and bound in Great Britain by Billing & Sons Ltd, Worcester.

JOHN STUBBINGS WEBB – MAIN EVENTS 1853 - 1860

Page	Date of letter	
16	23.3.53	Sailed for New York to represent Sheffield iron & steel manufacturer.
110	12.54	J.S.W. "takes run over to England".
112	17.1.55	J.S.W. married by brother to Mary Hannah Krauss in Manchester Cathedral.
115	7.3.55	J.S. & M.H. on board "America" S.S.
137	12.6.55	J.S.W.'s job in jeopardy.
127	11.9.55	"Coming events" render housekeeping desirable.
127	10.1.56	J.S. & M.H.W.'s first child, Evelyn Mary, born 15.12.55.
138	17.11.56	J.S.W. made redundant.
139	2.10.57	J.S. & M.H. start a school 1000 miles west of New York at Dundee, Illinois.
160	28.12.57	Their second child is born.
161	8.2.58	Their second child dies.
166	18.10.58	J.S.W. buys a schoolroom & plot a Dekalb, Illinois.
167	"	They build a house on to the school.
170	"	They start Dekalb Academy
179	"	Third child born 5.1.59. (my grandmother)

LIST OF ILLUSTRATIONS

This book is dedicated to my dear wife of fifty years (March 8th 1941) for her outstanding and unfailing helpfulness in bringing it into being.

ACKNOWLEDGEMENTS

I am very grateful to my friend Frank E. Dodman author of the Observer Books of Ships, etc. for the drawing of the Royal Mail Paddle Steamer 'Asia'.

Every effort has been made to trace the copyright holder of the article about the Siamese Twins. We would be grateful if the copyright holder would contact the publisher.

FOREWORD

Some years ago I expressed an interest in family history and my late uncle, Stanley Webb Davies, fetched down from his loft a box of letters, which he had rescued from his father's loft forty years earlier. The letters turned out to have been written by my great-grandfather, John Stubbins Webb, and these letters form the body of this book.

In 1853 John Stubbins Webb left his home and family in Sheffield where he had lived for all his twenty-eight years, and set sail for the United States of America on the Paddle Steamer "Asia". He wrote many letters to his parents, and some to his older brother, the Rev. G.M. Webb and sisters, Mary Ann and Susannah. In 1897, when J.S.W. was seventy-two and his brother and sisters were long dead, he also wrote, at the request of his daughter Ethel, then twenty-eight*, many long letters of family history and autobiography. These letters have been interwoven with the earlier ones, and the book begins with two of them, in which he speaks of his childhood and youth and preparation for leaving for the States.

The letters were written in good copper-plate handwriting on wafer-thin 'blued' paper, very like present day airmail paper except that it is less opaque. They were almost all crossed i.e. the pages written from top to bottom, turned through 90 degrees and written from top to bottom, and many were badly faded. The first reading proved to be a very laborious but, nevertheless, rewarding experience.

The oddities of expression, the spelling, punctuation, even the erratic use of capital letters and abbreviation, have generally been retained, but not the sparse use of paragraphing. Parts of the letters not thought to be of sufficient general interest have also been omitted – a row of dots indicates such an omission.

Though the numbering of the 1897 letters is not given, the numbering of the American letters is J.S.W.'s own.

---

* Ethel was to die of diptheria only four years later.

Dear Ethel,

I propose now to give you a sketch of my business career in England, a period of 14 years, 1838 – 1852. I was 13 years old in 1838; I think my father was rather staggered at my last half year's school bill of about £9, and thought me quite old enough to be earning, instead of costing money. Moreover he believed I should learn more in business than in school, and so far as commercial knowledge is concerned I certainly did. I also supplemented this by taking evening lessons, though rather in a desultory, off and on sort of way, in french and drawing and had good teachers in both. It was a thousand pities I did not make better use of them. My first essay in business was with my father, about 9 months from July, '38/Apl. '39. He had then a warehouse in George St. (Sheffield) and dealt with manufacturers in copper and sheet brass, and wire, paper (brown cap printing & tissue) copper ingots single and double plated with silver for rolling into sheets for silver plated ware, brass solder, etc. etc. It was a business which should have been profitable, but my dear father had a too easy going disposition to make a pushing business man, so this my first introduction to trade soon came to an end by my father's failure.

Before proceeding, I should like to introduce you to my father's man Wm Dunkley who acted as out porter etc. He was a discharged soldier, tall, thin & wiry. He taught me gun exercises and was full of interesting talk about his exploits. He lived with his married brother whose wife was somewhat of a shrew. Wm, the bachelor, often congratulated himself on his single blessedness, and would repeat Solomon's words with strong conviction "It is better to dwell in a corner of the housetop, than in a wide house with a brawling woman". On being thus turned adrift Mr Schofield found me employment for the succeeding seven weeks in his office, and at sales, as auctioneer's clerk. No wages were agreed on, and the payments were irregular. 20/- for two weeks, 10/- for 3 wks, 15/- for 2 wks; that is 45/- altogether. I mention this because it was the first money I had got, and the pride and pleasure I felt in giving the first sovereign to my mother has not since been equalled even by presents of £100. Let it be understood that my dear mother did not muzzle the ox on this occasion. My father was anxious for me to learn a trade, so he engaged me to Mr Turner of the Suffolk Works, as shopboy, where I was set to the uncongenial task of oiling knives which disgusted me so that I left the first week end. After about a week's interval, Joseph Ashmore, who was then courting my sister, Mary Ann, took me into his workshop. I was with him till Nov. 23/30 a period of 19 weeks. This was somewhat of a kindergarten experience. After leaving Joseph Ashmore I had no employment for about three months, till the middle of Feb. 1840 when my father succeeded in making an arrangement for me with Messrs Carter & Smith, of Eldon St. Brewery, which was destined to be of long endurance. I was their book-keeper and cashier 12½ years. Only one break occurred in all that time, and that was for three months from Jan 11/41 to April 14/41 during my brother's brief venture into business on his own account. You may think it unlikely, but it is no less strange than true, that my being now a total abstainer is chiefly due to my having been 12½ years in a brewery, and having occasionally to visit public houses on business. It was because of the possible danger of such associations, that I at the outset determined to abstain, and did so without taking any pledge. I did not like having to go to public houses in the town, but I had this unpleasant duty only when one of the travellers was ill and no-one else could take his place. The country journeys which part of the time I took alternate weeks were very enjoyable as there was seldom anyone in them but the landlord or landlady. These I did on horseback, covering 40-50 miles in the day. My favourite journey was in Derbyshire. Breakfasting at Ashompton Inn or "Lady Bower", as it is sometimes called, I would go along Darwen Moor to Hope, Bradwell and Eyam, Middleton Dale, Litton Dale, Hathersage, etc.

Mr Smith willingly lent me a horse when I wanted to ride for pleasure. Both he and his wife were invariably kind to me and he was very wroth with Mr Brown when he took me away to become his American agent. They were good religious people too and never seemed to harbour the least suspicion of wrongdoing in their trade. And I can also speak well for their men, who were with little exception very good fellows.

All the years I was at the Brewery I was a regular constant teacher at Eldon St. Sunday School. When we had tea parties or school treats a small barrel was sent from the Brewery to supply the hot water.

Yours affectionately

John S. Webb

My Dear Ethel,

Towards the close of my Sheffield career I had a very uncommon treat, viz. a visit with my dear sister Susan to the Great Exhibition in London in 1851, the first of its kind. It was not usual in those days in the industrial community to take, as a matter of course, an annual holiday trip to the seaside or elsewhere. The only pleasure trip I remember to have had was when my father drove mother and Susan and me to Ashover and Matlock, which filled my young mind with such delight that I dreamed about it for some time after. But London, wonderful London, was a veritable fairyland to me. There was a great rivalry between contending Railway Cos, consequently we had to pay only 5/- each for our return tickets from Sheffield to London!* One of my intimate friends in Sheffield was H.J. Moulson, and it was through him I made the acquaintance of James Moorhouse, now Bishop of Manchester. He little anticipated then the honour that awaited him. He afterwards became curate of the Parish Church and was bold enough to aspire to the hand of Dr Sale's, the vicar's, daughter, his present wife, whom he has eulogised. The vicar at that time did not think him good enough. Your mother blames me for not renewing my acquaintance, but I do not believe in unequal combinations, for as Goldsmith's Vicar of Wakefield truly said "Such as are poor, and will associate with none but the rich, are hated by those they avoid and despised by those they allow." Besides I have another reason which I may mention anon.

My brother George during this portion of my career and especially after he had commenced his college course, was very anxious for me to follow in his footsteps,** and urged me frequently to be diligent in my studies. I had a strong desire in that direction, but circumstances prevented me from accumulating the means. This difficulty he had a scheme to overcome, as you shall know.

It was in the middle of October 1852 that I left my kind employer, Mr Smith. He commissioned me to buy whatever I desired as a parting present from him, and would have me buy some additional article when

---

*   London – Sheffield 81 miles
**   Study for the ministry and be ordained

14

he saw my modest purchase. And now after 44 years use my dressing case and leather travelling desk serve to remind me of one whose memory I shall always esteem and respect though he *was* a brewer. Mrs Smith was exceedingly kind to Joseph Ashmore in his last illness, visiting him frequently, and rendering him much spiritual comfort.

And now I was to enter a new life; I at once began to attend at the Atlas Works, my business there for nearly four months being to learn all I could of the nature and the quality of the materials and goods in which I should have to deal. The Atlas Works here mentioned were not the immense place which Mr Brown afterwards built and called by the same name. At this time his manufactures were chiefly limited to cast steel, files, and conical buffers. In the new Works he gave up the files, and added Bessemer Steel and armour plates for ships. Making cast steel was an interesting and dangerous process. The pots were made of fireclay, which men kneaded with their feet, and had loose lids. The furnace was covered except where holes were left through which the pots were let into it. When the metal was melted to a white heat they were poured into ingot moulds, and afterwards rolled out. The difficulty of making a large casting from these little pots was great. Each man waited his turn and unless the pots were poured into the mould without interruption, there would be a flaw which would spoil the casting. I was looking on on such an occasion when one man let his pot slip from his long pincers, and the molten metal was spilt on the floor among the men's feet. The best beverage used by them for quenching thirst under excessive heat and perspiration is oatmeal and water. Having studied qualities and nomenclature and thus prepared myself for business, Mr Brown accompanied me to Liverpool in March 1853 and next day saw me on board the "Asia S.S." for New York .

With dear love,
Ever your affectionate
John S. Webb

No 1.   Asia Steam Packet, Atlantic Ocean
                                                    March 23rd. 1853

Dear Father and Mother,

Safe and sound so far, thank God, but still between 500 and 600 miles
from our destination. Up to this time have had a most favourable passage
excepting last Saturday night when we got a pretty good rocking several
being quite pitched out of their berths and your humble servant only
saving himself by keeping fast hold to the side of his berth. I have
suffered from sickness but not so much as I expected. For this reason I have
not been able to take any note of events. While labouring under it you feel
quite careless and indifferent to whatever occurs. I felt nothing the first
day but at nights my stomach and head began a consultation which soon
terminated in a quarrel in which the latter almost turned itself inside out.
Tuesday began very calm, the disagreement ceased awhile but soon broke
out afresh as a new cause of disturbance occurred. This state of things
continued till yesterday morning, when I bribed my poor aggrieved porter
with a couple of pills, which had such an effect on his temper and so
changed his tone that I was able to get up for breakfast for the first time. I
have been quite jolly ever since and have reason to believe I shall be, as I
have had a good seasoning. After all, a voyage is a tedious thing, though
it is easy to believe that men may not only become reconciled but even
prefer it. For my part give me the fields or roads or even the miry streets
on a dirty day and even the risk of chimney pots to the tender mercies of
the billows dashing against the side of my bedboard. But now for facts.
"The Asia" is very fine vessel of 2,200 tons including coal of which she
carries 1,000 tons for consumption on the passage. The Engine is 800
horsepower, her piston rods have a stroke of 8½ feet; the machinery is
very ponderous. Erected on the centre of the lower deck abaft the main
hatches are the cookhouse, bar, grand saloon, the berths, stores, hold etc.
below. Above these is the upper deck. On either side of the paddles are
the offices and workplaces of the purser, chief steward, baker, carpenter,
also the ice house and cowhouse for we have a cow which is brought out
under special contract to supply the necessary quantity of milk which is, I
assure you, of a good quality, too. The space unoccupied on the outside is
protected by strong bulwarks so that there is no fear of being washed

overboard. The ship's crew including officers amounts to 110 men and 60 passengers eleven of which are second class. The regular accommodation for the latter is good but unfortunately the quantity of freight on board is so great that the grand saloon was half filled and the back saloon completely so. Our bill of fare has included Turkey, Geese, Ducks, Fowls, Rabbits, Beef, Mutton, Veal, Ham, Eggs, Irish stew, Puddings, Pies, Tarts, Custards, Cheese, Cakes, Fish, Soup, Almonds, Raisins, Apples, Prunes Figs etc. etc. etc. so that with an appetite one might get quite fed up.

Paddle Steamer "Asia". 2,226 tons. 1850 - 1867.
The British and North American Royal Mail Steam Packet Company

March 24th 1853

A most beautiful morning after a calm night. Took a walk on deck last night after ten o'clock by moonlight, very pleasant. I proceed to detail the events and circumstances of our voyage. After clearing out of Liverpool we passed the "Marco Polo" which was to sail for Australia the following day. She is a fine vessel and thronged with people like a beehive. She carries between 600 and 700 passengers. She saluted us by the way. We left Cape Clear on Sunday afternoon about 4 o'clock. I could not help noticing the difference in the colour of the water which changed from green to deep indigo as we attained those parts of the ocean which are deemed unfathomable. The most beautiful sight, however, is the track in the rear of the vessel with its light green waves crested with foam and which extends as far as you can see. I was rather disappointed with regard to that extent, the horizon being very limited and the expanse having no mark by which you can judge the distance it appears less than it really is which I am informed is about 20 miles. I cannot compare it to anything so like as an immense moor. I have as yet seen none of the monsters of the deep, but gulls and divers in abundance. Our amusements on board consist of reading, conversation, singing, violin, cards, draughts, chess and shuffleboard. The latter is played on deck and is a fine game to promote digestion and circulation. It consists of a board chalked on the deck (see below). We stand at a distance and with a long handled wooden "shovel", slide the round flat bowls into the squares and of course try to push out our opponents.

	10	
6	1	8
7	5	3
2	9	4
	-10	

My messmates are from all quarters of the earth; Scottish, Irish, English, German, Spanish, Canadian and Statesmen. We form a very agreeable party. One poor fellow, a namesake to boot from Cornwall, a miner by profession whom a Yankee is taking out to seek copper in the States, has kept himself aloof, having dormouse-like lived in his berth nearly all the time on plea of sickness. His appetite has not however suffered any diminution. He has taken his meals regularly and perhaps with greater zest than any of the rest of us. We sent him from table one day what we thought would be a complete caulker. Two large plates containing a whole fowl two large slices of Beef and Ham, a quantity of Potatoes, Cabbage, a roll of Bread and a pint of Beer, all which he devoured with great relish. He has got the byname of Pickles from the quantity he ate the first day on board. There are two berths in each of our cabins. My berthmate is a Mr Wilson, a young Englishman residing in Toronto, Canada. He has invited me to call upon him when I go that way. Our daily progress has been from 8 – 12 knots an hour or from 190 – 200 miles a day. One gent has kept what he calls his log book which chiefly contains portraits taken on the sly of various persons on board. I should tell you that our day consists of 24½ hours as we gain about half an hour daily as we proceed westwards. On Sunday morning prayers were read in the grand saloon by Capt. Lott. It is very pleasant to hear the sailors all lustily chanting one of their simple rude ditties as they raise a sail. It is of famous service in keeping time or their spirits up when getting drenched to the skin by the heave seas which are sometimes shipped. We expect to meet the "African" which left New York yesterday.

New York March 26/53

Arrived safe and sound last night and feel at present rather perplexed at my novel position: everything to do without any idea of where I should commence, but hope to feel more settled in a day or two.

Excuse more at present

from, yours dutifully

J.S. Webb

No. 2 P   Mrs Dean 44 Sands St Brooklyn

April 2nd 1853

Dear Father and Mother,

I can't let this post pass without writing to you, seeing I have enclosed so many for my friends. The weather since my arrival has been delightful & the trees are already showing signs of the approaching spring, or rather of its presence. The thermometer has ranged from 56° to 64° so that as yet I have felt no inconvenience from either heat or cold. I am very comfortable and happy, have been fortunate in finding such a home as is seldom met with on this side of the Water. At 6 o'clock every morning the bell is rung to bid us rise, at a ¼ to 7 the second bell is rung, for family prayers, & at 7 the third for breakfast. At about 8 I sally out to New York, about 1 or 2 I proceed to an eating house for dinner. About 6 business is over except with the shopkeepers, & I return to Brooklyn to tea. After that I either have a game of chess, with one of my Sheffield friends or I write my letters, or muster the information I have acquired during the day, & put it in order; or I go to see some of the Lions of the place, so that with one thing or other I do not feel the isolation, and time passes swiftly and pleasantly away. I find many things very strange, especially the manner of living; there is not that homeliness, so delightful to an Englishman. The food also is of a different character. Many of the dishes are a mystery to me. We have India corn cake, which is delightful, stewed lobsters & clams, smoked mackerel, cold raw cabbage, iced water. The cooking is very good, pastry excellent & abundance but you must pay for it. Mrs Dean keeps an excellent table. We have fish & meat to breakfast and tea & if we go home to dinner we find profusion, including fruit but no liquors. The charge is 25 cents extra for dinner, about the same as we should pay in New York. Everything is laid out in style; dinner napkins etc. to boot. Our common parlour would vie with some of the best drawing rooms in Sheffield & the situation of the house is pleasing and healthful .

. . . .

Mr Brown will enclose for you; give my kind regards to all enquiring friends, and accept my best love yourselves.

from

Your affectionate son

J.S.Webb

No. 3   Mrs Dean's, 44 Sands Street, Brooklyn

King's County, Long Island

April 8th 1853

Dear Parents,

I never felt so much pleasure in writing to my relatives and friends as now that I am so far separated from them. To me the distance seems to draw them nearer. I hope the feeling is mutual.

. . . .

Mrs Dean is the widow of an officer, ladylike in her manner and careful in her choice of boarders. They are consequently respectable and desirable acquaintances. She leaves this house for a larger on 1st May. I expect to accompany her but am not quite sure. She has many applications, some having a prior claim, but she has promised to accommodate me if possible.

Candles are never used. Camphine* lamps take their place and are

---

* Probably kerosene with camphor additive

in, my opinion, an excellent substitute. There is one placed in each chamber which can be lit whenever wanted with a lucifer match.

Each boarder has a key of the front door and whenever, for pleasure or business, expects to be out late, he puts his name on a slate hung up in the hall. On his return he wipes it out again and it is the duty of the person whose name only remains to put out the light and fasten the door. Everything is done with such order and regularity that the most fastidious person would be satisfied.

There is a great variety of religious sects here. Upwards of eighteen in Brooklyn and thirty in New York. Of the latter ten are Jewish synagogues and twenty-two Roman Catholic Churches. I have hitherto attended the same place as Mr Sawyer in Washington St. held by the Methodist Episcopalians and am much pleased with the minister, Dr Kennedy. Mr Sawyer is personally acquainted with him and has promised to introduce me. I do not intend to leave our own church for all that. I prefer our beautiful liturgy to all their prayers, and however excellent, proposed going to St Ann's a church in the immediate neighbourhood which Mrs Dean attends, and Mr Sands also, to whom I had a letter from Mr Moss.

I despatched at dinner today a great dish of oysters from which I should have recoiled with horror at home. My appetite has been excellent since I got the better of my seasickness, nothing has come amiss to it . . . . . .
. . . .

We have preserved peaches, but by and bye I guess we shall have plenty of raw fruit, and then I shall not wish them. There are pineapples in the market but they are hardly yet in season. Bananas are also abundant. Says I to a man selling them, "What do you ask?" "Four cents each," says he . . .
. . . .

The bread is skilfully made up into the shape of a large ear of wheat, showing the grains and is consequently all Kissing crust. It is seldom cut but broken into pieces of convenient size.

With much love to yourselves & every member of the family,

I remain your ever affectionate son,

J. S. Webb

No. 4   44 Sands St. Brooklyn
                                                  April 21/53

Dear Parents,

The arrival of the "Arabia" steamer yesterday inspired me with the hope that I would receive news of home, though there was scarcely time for my letters to be answered as she left Liverpool on the 9th. I was disappointed and shall have to wait above a week longer for the Canada, when if all my correspondents are prompt in answering I shall have a budget of eleven letters responding to those of mine, which will have been received before the vessel started on 16th. Oh what a delectable feast it will be. I hope you will not fail to write every week. I feel quite envious of my friends when I see them bringing home a bundle of letters by nearly every steamer. I am sure I deserve this at the hands of my correspondents .
. . . .

I feel now settled down – that is till nine days more elapse . . . That is the great moving day in New York and neighbourhood. Every article of furniture seems alive. All the carts in the city are engaged in this great *flitting*. The origin of this practice, according to the current legend, is that in olden times, when on the present site of New York there were only two houses, the residents felt a great desire for a change and the wish being mutual they agreed to remove into each other's house. This happened on the first of May. On the same day at the end of the year they moved back again, and as the place increased in size the practice continued. I will not vouch for the truth of this story.

Fires are a very frequent occurrence; scarcely a night but one or two occur. Indeed they are so common that the church bells cannot be rung for service in the same straightforward manner as with us, that being the way in which the alarm is given. There is a man continually on the lookout night and day, on the tower of the City Hall here and in New York, to give notice by tolling the great bell attached to each of those edifices. The alarm is taken up by the church bells of the district in which the fire happens even if only a small one, and by all the bells in the city if a large one. Each district is numbered and it can instantly be told in what vicinity the fire has broken out by the number of strokes in succession. There was a large fire in the Navy yard the other day, damage $25,000, and last night in a timber, or as they are called, lumber yard in Brooklyn. The engines are very powerful, effective and well manned. They are almost the first on the spot and with the assistance of the hook and ladder company very soon subdue the raging element. There is great emulation amongst them, and all means are tried by each company to obtain a favourable notice in the next day's paper.

Mrs Stowe's* visit to England is looked upon with an evil eye. She is looked upon as a traitor to her country and great bitterness is sometimes expressed. The general plea in favour of slavery is that the slaves are better off than if they were free, and certainly if the same system were pursued in their emancipation as in Jamaica it might be attended with the same disastrous consequences. The English are charged with enslaving and selling Chinese at the present time. Mrs Stowe is charged with having slandered and vilified the character of a Dr Parker, an eminent clergyman, attributing sentiments which he never uttered. Be that as it may they lay themselves open to the same charge, when they assert that her book is a mass of lies. The negroes in New York are very numerous and appear to be an intelligent body of men capable of rising when they have opportunity; some are well dressed and 'ape the gentleman'.

I see the Sheffield papers and have read to the 9th April. It was a matter of congratulation that the Irish were inclined to emigrate and improve their condition in a foreign land. What quantities do I see wherever I go! The servants in our house are all from the Emerald Isle and fresh arrivals may be seen going along the streets of the city from the ships in great bodies, isolated by their peculiar nationality from the surrounding multitude, like a drop of oil in water. But this I see from the paper is going on to an alarming extent so that labourers cannot be obtained or tempted to stay for four times the usual hire.

The ladies were shocked at the tea table by the abrupt manner in which certain interesting news from England was announced by one of our boarders. He observed, he said as he came home, that the newsboys had a nice bit of news to tell. The ladies said, "What is it?" He objected to tell them but when pressed he imitated the tone of the boys and said "Arrival

---

* *Uncle Tom's Cabin* by Harriet Beecher Stowe was published March 20, 1852

23

of Arabia Queen Victoria got *another* [*] baby". It sounded so droll that a general laugh succeeded the blushes.

The town (Sheffield) will lose a learned man in the removal of Dr Jacob to his new appointment as headmaster at Christ's Hospital,[**] , though it could scarcely be bestowed on a worthier man.

I propose writing to my old associates and scholars in Eldon St. next week, to be read on Whitmonday, that they may have something to remind them of me on that pleasant occasion when I would give a good deal to be present with them. I have not given up the work, though I have refused for the present to accept any permanent post, not yet having joined any particular church.

Those infatuated people, the Spirit Rappers, are very numerous and amongst them may be found men of high standing. Judge Edmunds, a man of learning and integrity and much respected, makes no secret of his having sought assistance and advice from the spirits of great men of all the ages in deciding difficult matters. I find they are not altogether unknown in England though I have heard nothing of them while there.

My friend Littlewood has received a most interesting letter from Wm. Harmer containing a journal of the dangers and labours he experienced in the passage to California. I extract an account of San Francisco:-

"The earliest mention of this place was 1776 when two missionaries from the Romish Church named Benito Camboni and Francisco Palon arrived in this bay and established a point for civilising the native tribes. They were Spaniards but came here from Mexico. A few wooden houses only were erected at that time. The settlement was named Yerba Buena, or Good Herbs and was so called until occupied by the Americans. The commerce of the place was in hides and tallow. In 1846 there were 150 inhabitants. About this time the Americans began to emigrate [sic] and the Indians were driven off. The population increased in two years to 500. Yerba Buena, now called San Francisco, stands on a narrow neck of land between the bay and the ocean, fronting eastwards on the bay, and the ocean 5 miles to the west. Standing on Telegraph Hill to the north of the

[*] her 8th in 13 years; Prince Leopold b. 7.4.1853

[**] a famous school in England

city you can see the bay, 8 miles wide, crowded with ships from all parts of the world, beyond is the coast of Contra Costa with its new city of Oakland, beyond which rises hill above hill to the Redwood Forest, on the summits towering over is the conical peak of Mount Diabolo, at a distance of 30 miles; to the north is the entrance from the ocean.

"In 1846 war with Mexico gave an impulse to commerce, requiring shipments of supplies for military purposes. On March 13th 1847 there were in the harbour 6 vessels. In 1847 the number of inhabitants exclusive of Indians was 375. The first school was opened April 3rd 1847. In May 1847 a public meeting was called to erect a place of worship. At this time there were 50 houses. In January 1847 the name of the town was changed to San Francisco. The first gold was discovered near Sutter's Foot, 30 miles from Sacramento or New Helvetia as it was then called, in December 1847. Adventurers and merchandise from all nations now began to pour in. Buildings were vacated, all leaving for the mines. Labour, which had been but $2 per day, now could seldom be had for $20. In the first two months of the golden age the amount of dust brought into San Francisco was $250,000, and the next two months $600,000. In September 1848, the first vessels arrived here from New York. The first brick building was raised Sept. 1848. the first elected minister was the Rev. I.D. Hunt, at a salary of $2,500 per year. Dec. 1st '48 flour sold at $27* per barrel, beef $20, pork $60, butter $1 per pound, and cheese at 70 cents. In Feb. 1849, the population was 2,000, in July /49 3,614 persons arrived, in Sept. 5,802, and in Oct. 4,000 arrived. In Jan. 1850 3 females were sold to pay their passage to this port for five months at $15 each, the captain pocketing the money. In 1849, 50,000, in 1850 65,000 emigrants arrived. The first fire broke out May 4th 1850, destroyed 400 houses valued at $4,000,000. Houses were soon rebuilt but in June was another great fire, 300 houses destroyed, $3,000,000 property consumed.

"In July 1850 there were seven churches or meeting-houses. The principal part of the city was constantly being burnt down until 1852 when bricks and stone began to be used. Large quantities of stone is brought from China. There are now some very handsome buildings. A population of about 50,000. A splendid business. Expenses enormous but profits are in

---

* $1 was worth 4/2d. or 21p i.e. 5 dollars to the pound sterling

accordance. Board here is $20 per week generally. I am paying $18. Washing is $4; if done by Chinese $3 or $3.50. For hair cutting I paid $1. Some places charge 50 cents. Society is good, indeed everything has much the appearance of the Eastern Cities, New York, etc. The climate is delightful, one temperature the year round. I am quite well and feel quite sure I shall like the place as a residence for a time and have no doubt shall be repaid so far as money is concerned; all I think I want now is a wife."

From the foregoing account you may notice that however extraordinary the increase in population may be here, they beat us hollow in the far west. Not all the dangers of the way, the horrid yellow fever of which so many died, nor the murderous character of the natives of Granada can stop the thirsty search for gold. Vessels are constantly leaving this port for the auriferous[*] regions crowded with passengers. That in which Harmar sailed to Panama had 800 steerage and 300 cabin passengers, about 37 of whom were conveyed by Charon's Ferry to a very different haven to the one which they expected to reach.

Poor Harmar lost all his baggage but a hat-box and small trunk. A large box which contained a valuable stock of clothes with many things which money could not replace were all lost in lowering it into the boat. It broke to pieces and dropped into the sea. He jumped into the water to save a small tin box containing some valuables and grasped what he took to be it, but found it only a box of cigars.

I remain yours as ever

J. S. Webb

[*] gold yielding

Of the last half page on which Letter No. 4 is written, half is given to a pencil drawing inscribed 'New York University, Washington Sq.' the rest to this table of population growth. T.B.D.

Population of the City of New York		Brooklyn	
Year	Number	Year	Number
1677	2,000	1810	4,402
1730	8,638	1820	7,175
1790	22,589	1830	15,396
1840	312,712	1840	36,233
1850	517,849	1850	96,860
1853	570,000	1853	105,000
		Williamsburg	
		1835	3,328
		1840	5,094
		1845	11,338
		1850	30,856
		1853	42,000

the latter city almost joins Brooklyn

Letter No. 5 is written on a sheet of paper folded to quarto, of which the first half page is taken up by a steel engraving of New York and Brooklyn, shown as if from the air. It is of the 'tuppence coloured' variety. This paper was clearly produced for immigrants and visitors to send home. T.B.D.

No. 5

> Mr Cottier's, 79 Cranberry Street,
> Brooklyn, Long Island
> Office 15 Gold St., New York
> May 7th 1853

Dear Parents,

I need not tell you how delighted I was to hear from you. Mother's letter, No. 1 of April 13th came to hand on Monday and the little scrip of

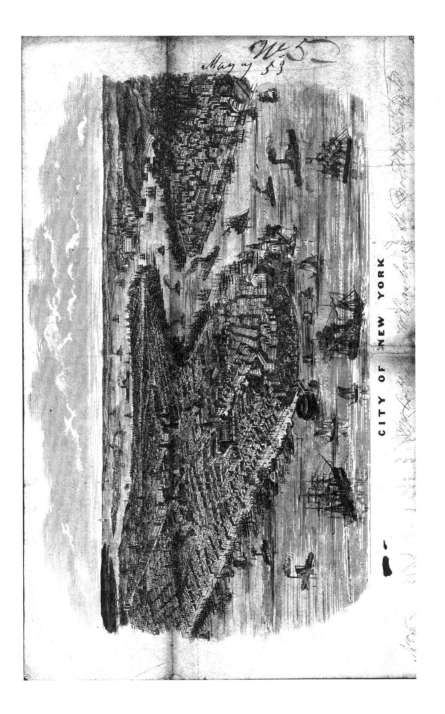

CITY OF NEW YORK

Steel engraving of New York City

the 22nd on Thursday. The delay in receiving the first was caused by its being directed to Brooklyn. By some extraordinary mismanagement, the mails do not come over from N.Y. for several days. I am sorry that you should have been anxious about my unworthy self and at the same time think I had the most cause for trembling and that I did so will be proved by the manner in which my first letter was written. My sickness was unpleasant to bear, but proved beneficial afterwards in improving my appetite. If they had brought me stewed snakes or boiled lizards to eat on my landing, I should have fallen to with satisfaction, and even now I think I could relish two or three frogs! Indeed, if I had possessed no better appetite here than I had at home, I should have been starved by prejudice. The food is not inferior, but the manner of serving is so different. For instance, for breakfast (I know you like particulars) I sit down to table, spread the napkin on my knees, and cutting a lump of butter from the dish, I place it on a little plate, for my exclusive use. I then look round to choose my bread, either brown or white loaf . . . or Indian corn bread which is delicious as hot breakfast buns or some kind of fancy bread, as sweet or light cakes are called. Having got some I butter it myself, have a cup of tea or coffee handed to me and next consider whether I shall have a piece of that nice steak, or that fine smoked mackerel – delicious. I had one or two of those little round savoury sausages or some of the sweetmeats, or much – or little – of each. A jolly breakfast is it not, but remember it has to support nature from 7 a.m. to 1 or ½ past. I then go to business for as I have commenced the day I may as well proceed according to your wish.

Well, I cross the ferry, with numbers of others on the same errand, but most of them with a clearer view of the day's occupation than myself, and until last Thursday when I took possession of my office, I assure you I have had a very weary time of it. With a map of the district in which I wished to move copied on a card, I have had to walk hither and thither in search of a location and customers, often going miles out of my way during the day for want of a better acquaintance with the place, and after taking the trouble to copy a long list out of last year's directory and put the streets in order, find half of them removed and many others at the very far end of streets from the place I had entered them. Then, tired to death, and vexed beyond endurance, I turn into the office of one or other of my friends, fearing all the time that they will vote me a great bore. Of course these are evils which time will remove and this fact helps me to bear them; already they begin to disappear, and every day puts them at a greater distance. You have no idea what a difficulty it has been to find a suitable office. It was necessary to have it in a certain location or I might as well be without. All the trades are classified. In one street you will find little else but dry goods or drapery, in another hardware, another shipping stores, another bankers' exchange offices, etc. or stationery and fancy goods and so forth. There are exceptions but this is the rule. Then when I met with one, up one or even two flights; the rent asked was so enormous as to preclude all thought of taking it. One place in which I could scarcely turn round was $200, another, a little larger and both upstairs, $350. I have been asked $1200 for one room on the ground floor. But to proceed with the day, though you will excuse this digression as I introduced you first where you could sit down and rest with me.

By & bye, the earth being on the move as well as myself, in due course he presents New York to the sun and people begin to think of their dinner. The question is, where shall I go, to Clark and Brown's in Maiden Lane, or that French house in Water St. or Goslings in Nassau St. where a turtle is generally lying under sentence of death just outside the door and thinking of its protracted absence from home and wondering where it is. It remains in happy ignorance of its fate. Shall I pass him by and call on Monday for a share of the veritable soup for which I shall be charged a 1/- or 1/6, and go now to that place under the exchange where I had such a nice cup of chocolate the other day, or shall I go down into one of the numerous oyster saloons which open their mouths ready to receive the hungry multitude, who after feeding on their entrails, are disgorged like Jonah from their bellies. The perplexity as to where you shall dine in New York is not because you cannot find a place, but from the choice and variety of places. The first I mentioned is the great resort of our Sheffield men, but I do not like it. I prefer the French houses. I will take you into one, Gosling's for instance. If you enter the ground floor you see numbers of gents discussing oysters in all forms, but as I want dinner I go upstairs. I enter a spacious saloon nicely fitted up with mirrors and the floor occupied with small tables, each covered with a clean, white cloth on which stands a cruet, a bottle of water and a basin of ice; five or six chairs are placed round. But let us go to one of those snug little ones with only two chairs and have it all to ourselves. Well, what are we to have? Look at that little book of fare, printed in French and English. There are many things which you will not like to call for, on account of your utter ignorance as to what they are. Let us have some Beef *á la Mode.* You order it from the waiter who comes up to you before you have had time to read above the first two or three articles on the list. He steps up to a corner, tells the man standing there, who in turn repeats the order through a speaking tube to the regions below where the Cyclops are making better use of their furnaces than by forging thunderbolts. Presently the object of desire is handed up and brought to you by the waiter, who during the interval has brought you plate, knife and fork, spoon and butter. After dispatching the first course you think what shall be next. Well suppose we try a Jenny Lind pudding with claret sauce. It is very good and cooling, much like our blancmange. After you have finished that, just wash it down with a little more of that iced water and let us be off. (There is no dinner hour here). Now go up to the bar at the side, tell them what you have had and pay for it. Here is one good trait in the New York people (not Yankees, they are in the New England states) that they believe in honour and act on the supposition that you possess it. The plan at some of the eating houses of placing a small check ticket on the table along with the dishes is preferable. Now come along, don't sit there as if you were at home, don't you see that the chairs are nearly all occupied and folks are still pouring in.

, Now to business again until 6 o'clock. That hour arrived, we will go down to Fulton Ferry, have you a cent, get it ready for the fare. Don't want change now for the crowd will be great and you must not stop up the road. Off we go. There is a nice breeze which makes the sloops and brigs walk away at a fine pace. What a splendid vessel that is. She is "Queen of Clippers", a sort of fast sailers in which the Americans excel. Look to your right, there in the midst of the stream, rides in solitary grandeur another Clipper ship, the "Sovereign of the Seas" from California whose guns told us of her arrival last night. As we approach the other side the passengers, many of whom have been seated in the cabins for a brief space, come to the front, some anxious to be home – get outside the chains to be ready to jump off as soon as the boat comes near the landing place. Off we go up the Fulton St. with the living stream and turn off the road to the right up Henry St. and then a few paces on Cranberry St. Before we go in let me tell you how I got here. I have already informed you of the removal of my former landlady to her new house and of my intention to proceed with them. I went up to the new house in Remson St. to which she is gone, last

31

Saturday and found to my great disappointment that the room appropriated to me was a most uncomfortable one in the roof, which slanting down part of its length left room for two *short* windows, close to the floor, so that looking out was impossible except by crouching down to their level. I therefore and Littlewood (who had and still has a bed in the same room as myself) were quite dissatisfied and near as time was, commenced looking out for new lodgings. He fortunately found a jeweller – an Englishman in New York who was going to a house too large and more expensive than he wished. The fact is he had been seeking a house about $500 and could not find a suitable one under $650, which his wife persuaded him to take, saying she would be at the trouble of providing for one or two boarders to make up the difference. We fortunately came in just at the nick of time and though I still remember my lodgings in Sand St. with pleasure and without finding the least fault, yet I like these better and am quite at home. They are homely religious people with a very nice daughter, a young lady of seventeen or eighteen. If you want to know what she is like you must imagine Mrs R. Staniforth at the same age. Their eldest son is gone to Australia – another is at home and there are also three girls and a boy. I was delighted to see some children in the house, the more so as the pleasure is not marred by their presence at meals. I soon became familiar with them all. Little Johnny in particular, who is quite as mischievous as Johnny's usually are.

Now let us go in. We will go upstairs and wash our hands and face and brush our hair and put our slippers on, young men on their preferment must be careful of such things where ladies are in the house, you know. Look, is this not a snug chamber? Here are two windows fronting to the street. Observe those fine trees close to the house, growing out of the pavement. That brick building opposite to the right with the tower is Henry Ward Beecher's lecture room (Mrs Stowe's brother), behind it, fronting the next street, in his church, also of brick. Look the other way to the corner of Henry St., there is the armoury; between the two are houses similar to our own. Now glance round the room. Between the windows is a bureau surmounted by a mirror, the drawers contain such things as we are using; our trunks and boxes are stowed into a closet. On one side of the drawers is a gas bracket and table. On the other, under the window, is a chair. Opposite the door is my bedstead of walnut with a hair mattress which I find much pleasanter than feathers. Between the head and the wall is my washstand. On the same side as the door is Mr Littlewood's bed with foot to the windows between which is his washstand. The other side is occupied with the fireplace which will however, be unnecessary as the room will be heated in winter by hot air. My black trunk and writing case and another chair fill up the inventory of larger goods. On the chimney piece is my accordion at one end, dressing case at the other and between is what Mr Littlewood calls his family picture gallery, consisting of a sister, brother and his wife, and mother. You know the latter, I am sure (late of High St.) Hung over these is a coloured French engraving of a pretty girl with a little dog in her arms, framed and glazed. Between the chimney and the window hangs my father's black portrait, and underneath Elizabeth and Susan.[*] On the table is my chess board and men which are often in requisition (I was teaching Miss Cottier last night). The floor is covered with a very good and pretty carpet. The blinds are a fancy pattern and taking all things into consideration it is as snug a place as any in New York or Brooklyn. From many sources I learn that many young men pay double or more for worse accommodation and without any of the home comforts I enjoy. The terms are $3½ per week, including lodging, breakfast and tea, and on Sunday, dinner, with gas and hot air. At Mrs Dean's I should have had to pay $4 per week, 25 cents for gas and find my own fuel. Even the latter is a consideration with Anthracite coal at $5 per 1,000 lbs. and bituminous coal such as you use $11 per 1,000 lbs. I should have had to pay the same whether there or abroad. At Mr Cottier's I shall only pay $1½ per week when from home. I find I have enlarged so much to save you the trouble of asking questions that I have not room to finish the day. We have been so long in the chamber that it is seven o'clock and the bell rings for tea, which I need not describe as it is the counterpart of breakfast. That over, we have family prayers and spend the evenings in reading or conversation, or music and singing. There is both a piano and a seraphine.[**] Or we go to some lecture or amusement.

The weather is fine on the whole but very wet yesterday.

I am yours with much love,

John S. Webb

[*] nieces of J.S.W.
[**] A sort of harmonium TBD.

My Father's Black Portrait

Letter No. 6 is missing.

No. 7   City Hotel, Baltimore June 4th '53

Dear Father and Mother,

   I have been wandering about this city and am come in to dine. But finding I am too soon I sit down to write to you and try to get cool. I came here by a very pleasant route; by cars to Frenchtown from Philadelphia and forward by the steamer "Genl. McDonald" down from Chesapeake Bay. The country through which the railway passes is very fine, it abounds with trees. There are extensive apple and peach orchards and the wheat is nicely shot, the clover in flower, the potatoes and Indian corn well up, flowers abundant; everything at the season looks cheerful, influenced alike for good by the bright sun and the passing shower. May this be your experience also.

   I do not like Baltimore as well as Phila., the latter I prefer to New York. I looked in the directory for the parties mentioned by Father but was confused by the number of the same names. I could not therefore choose them out with any certainty. There is an I.R. Paxson, but he is an attorney and most likely a son or nephew of your friend. My stay was so short that I could not make any calls of discovery.

   The trees, whose shade is so delightful, are also a source of annoyance. Caterpillars in great numbers, luxuriate in the foliage and their whole time not being occupied by eating, they amuse themselves by spinning down upon the pedestrians. I was passing along a street, full of thought, when I was aroused from my reverie by one of these gentlemen wriggling about inside my collar.

   A dark cloud hung over Baltimore at the time we approached it and broke in a thunderstorm just as we got to the basin. This, you are no doubt aware, is a slave state. There are upwards of 28,000 coloured people in Baltimore, of whom about 2,800 are slaves. There is a hostile feeling between the Northern and Southern States, chiefly on account of the slavery question. On this ground, the Southern people are doing all in their power to render themselves independent of the Northern, I mean so far as regards the manufacture of their own produce. Their darling scheme in Baltimore is to have a direct steam line of their own to Europe. The keel

35

for the first boat is already laid and there is no doubt that it will be an immense benefit to them.

The great show of this place is the Washington Monument from the top of which a splendid view of the city is seen.

All the waiters at this hotel are negroes.

I leave here tonight at half past six for New York.

The heat here is very great and the flies troublesome. I shall be glad to get away and do not care if I never come again. I hope there are home letters waiting for me in New York. I look for them every mail.

The Saratoga waters are very refreshing; they are flavoured with strawberry, raspberry, sarsaparilla etc. and are drank [sic] in an effervescent state. Milk and water is also very refreshing, only take care the water is frozen before it is put in the glass; this is generally drank [sic] after breakfast and tea, it prevents the heat consequent from taking those old fashioned beverages.

No. 7 continued

New York, June 6th 1853

Dear Parents,

I arrived from Philada. at 12.20 this noon. I left Baltimore at ½ p 7 Saturday night but the cars did not run through so I had to spend Sunday in Phila. I did not get there till about ½ to 1 a.m. I put up at the United States Hotel opposite the Mint in Chestnut St. near Independence Hall. I felt very lonely yesterday but passed the time as well as I could.

In the morning I went to the Revd. Albert Barnes' church opposite Washington Square. He is the author of the commentary which bears his name. It was Sacrament Sunday and the text was appropriate. "Do this in remembrance of me, etc." It was administered in what was to me a novel manner. After an address on the nature and intention of the ordinance, the minister held up a loaf of bread or rather biscuit and broke a piece, then the deacons or whatnot each took a loaf on a silver plate and went with it from pew to pew, each person breaking off a portion; the cup was conveyed in like manner. After service I enjoyed a turn round the squares, Washington and Independence.

In the afternoon, not knowing where to go, I observed others and amongst the pedestrians I saw a great number of coloured people, mostly going in one direction. I followed them to see what they were after, until we came to a church into which great numbers were pouring. I passed by until the time of commencement and then in I went. Never did I see such a lot of black faces because the place was crowded, the galleries occupied chiefly by children. They put themselves about to find me a seat which, when I had obtained it, I began to look where I was. Sure enough, there were the black sheep, I knew them by their wool but as the saying is "there are both black and white niggers". I believe, judging from their deportment, there was many a black face here belonging to a soul washed clean in the blood of the Lamb. There were some faces there very comely and there was also every variety of shade. The sleek and fine textured hair of one showed him to be of Spanish blood while the face of another vied with the coat in colour and was surmounted by veritable wool which the comb could never make straight. The preacher was a fine intelligent negro and it happened to be his farewell sermon. He preached a sermon which might have put many a pale face preacher to the blush, from the text "I commend you to God and to the word of His grace". The negroes are very excitable and there was such a scene after the sermon as I shall never forget. You cannot conceive the power which the affections and passions have over this poor race. It appeared as if some were taken in hysterics or convulsions. They would rise with outstretched arms and upturned eyes and after dilating themselves to the utmost would writhe and dance and scream till you would be ready to run for a doctor. One poor creature with a satin Quaker bonnet continued in this state till even her own people thought she was over-doing it and began to pull her shawl and induce her to sit down. The singing was beautiful and a most pleasing scene presented itself at the end of the service. One of the elders rose and proposed that a subscription should be made to show their regard for their departing friend. They all pressed forward with their mites anxious thus to show their love for him.

At night I went to a German Reformed Church in Sassafras St. and turned into bed in good time.

Thanks for your good wishes.

With much love I remain affectionately Jno. S. Webb

37

No. 8

Dear Parents,

I wrote to you last from Baltimore the extreme southern limit of my travels and now from the farthest north west to which I intend at present to extend my journey. I left Hamilton at 7 o'clock this morning by steamer "City of Rochester" for Leweston, arrived there, a distance of 45 miles, at 12 o'clock, proceeded by stage coach 7 miles to Manchester, which is close to the Falls on the American side. The view there is very poor compared to that obtained on the Canada side which presents the whole in its grandeur at once. Being informed of this beforehand I went direct to the ferry boat by which you must understand not such a Leviathan as we have at New York but a little cockleshell into which however they managed to stow about nine or ten persons. It is impossible to row directly across, from the force of the current. The banks on both sides are precipitous and a trifle higher than the falls so that to reach the ferry you have to descend a flight of about 300 steps or, if preferred, be lowered down an inclined plane with chain and pulley. At the opposite bank a road has been made from the landing place and is so steep that the horses can scarcely get up. We got into a coach but instead of going up we were backed down and expected to be backed into the river. One lady began to scream and begged her husband most piteously to take her out, which he did only just in time to prevent a fit. We at last got to the hotel which is a princely place, one of the best I have seen. It was now 2 o'clock. After washing and looking about a bit we dined at 3 o'clock. Mr Barton, brother to the lame Barton at the dramshop was there with his wife. After dinner I took a stroll, stood upon the table-rock at this end of the Horseshoe Falls so close to the cataract that the water washed my boots. I then went down by the side of the stream above the fall, picking my steps amongst the loose boulders and not a little amused at the quantities of bull-heads (alias tadpoles) and minnows which sported at the edge. There is a deal of fish of very decent size called bass. Amongst other things of interest I saw quantities of lobster shells all complete about 3 or 4 inches long which had been cast off to allow increased growth. One only I found at home in his shell but he was either dead or dormant for I could not persuade him to move. I climbed up the bank at a place where it appeared feasible, but wished myself back again when I got near the top which I thought I should never reach, it was so steep. I at last succeeded and continued my walk. I stopped at a cottage door where two men were smoking their pipe and spoke to them, was offered a chair which I gladly accepted. After resting a while I went back to my hotel to tea which we had at seven. Took a walk in the evening with a Scotsman whose acquaintance I had made and finished the night with conversation, the newspaper and writing to my dear father and mother.

A short time since a steamboat was drifted to the edge of the falls and stuck there for several weeks but at last was dashed over the abyss. A poor fisherman in his boat was likewise carried over the edge. He had lain down in the bottom of his boat and gone to sleep. It got into the current which carried him to the falls. He was observed to rise just at the moment it arrived at the brink, clasped his hands together and both disappeared. A young gent and his lady were standing at the edge of the precipice when jokingly he touched her. She started forward, he attempted to save her and both were lost in the foaming billows. A young lady also lost her life by losing her balance in gathering a flower on the brink and was dashed to pieces on the rocks below.

8 continued.   The American Hotel, Buffalo, N.Y.   June 20th

I slept so soundly after writing the foregoing that I trespassed far upon Sunday. I had wound up my watch too tight and stopped it, so did not know how time was progressing. When I got downstairs I found to my surprise and dismay that it was quarter past 10. Fortunately I was in time for breakfast as that meal is taken between 8 and 11 o'clock. I despatched it hastily and then went out to seek a church. I walked about a mile to the village and found the Episcopal Church closed, but a little further on I heard the songs of Zion in the strange land. It proceeded from the Presbyterian Church, a real country place of worship filled with tanned manly faces and rustic belles. The preacher's coat looked as if his wife had made it, so wrinkled and clumsy did it sit. My friend, Mr Logan, the Scotchman, came in and helped the village choir no end with his stentorian lungs. We then returned to lunch after which I took a turn near the Falls until dinner. After dinner I went to the Methodist Church near the other but dinner had occupied such a prodigious time that though service commenced at 4, I only came in for the fag end of the sermon which however was worth going to hear. I strolled further into the country and must have made a circuit of about 7 miles before I took tea. After tea, I followed the course of the river below the Falls till the failing light warned me to return. This is by far the prettiest road in the neighbourhood. The banks presented a face of rock with trees grown at the bottom and from the clefts and ledges. The tops of the tallest trees are considerably below the road. Creepers of various sorts amongst which the vine is most conspicuous, help to cover the rugged sides. Here and there you catch a glympse [sic] of the foaming cataract, crested and surrounded by trees. The other side of the road is also well wooded. Oh how I longed to have you with me, that I might show you the various beauties of the place. I retired early to bed for I felt tired and wished to rise early. I had heated myself so much and the night was close that I was long before I could sleep. I was completely saturated with perspiration and rose at quarter to 5 and was crossing the ferry at 6 a.m. – a little snake in the water about 12 or 14 inches long – and allowed myself to be drawn up by the machine as I did not choose to walk up so many steps. I was off to Buffalo at 7 a.m. where I arrived at ½ past 8 – 22 miles.

I have already finished my business here and am waiting the train for Troy, my next destination . . . .

I started at 5 o'clock P.M. to Troy, a nice little journey and rather more than 320 miles. I reached that city at ¼ p.6 this morning after travelling all night. I felt rather sleepy and stupid as I entered my hotel, "Troy House" but all was dissipated on receiving a packet of 12 home letters. What a feast! Breakfast served as dessert only. . . . .

And now with an assurance of my filial love I am, as ever,

Your affectionate son,
J.S. Webb

79 Cranberry St. Brooklyn July 8/53

Dear Parents,

I am now rich in home letters and have three of your own to answer. .
. . . .

I escaped your winter nicely. The people here would hardly believe about the late snow. I hope the fruit trees have not suffered from it. The mosquitoes are yet very few in number, and do not seem to care much for me. My friend Sawyer is much more annoyed by them and I do not think he bears the heat as well as myself. But the worst has yet to come. I shall lose some dripping when the mercury creeps from 80 – 90, then to 100 and 110° in the shade. We have had it 96° already. Tell M.A. that there is not the slightest probability of a war, though the Irish did kick up a bit of a row on the 4th. The Hibernian Society were having a procession through the city when they were stopped by a stage crossing their line. The marshall ordered him to back but he either would not or could not. On the stage jumped several of the hot-headed boys, dragged the driver down and beat him within an inch of his life, and then set on to fight two batches of police who had entered the field of Battle. The Irish were at last mastered and many taken prisoners. Two hostile companies of firemen, also attempted to persuade one another of their respective merits by appealing to arms and on the 4th July an immense quantity of gun powder and fireworks were exploded in defiance of the English and in commemoration of their glorious achievements over them. But for all this *we,* that is the Americans are a peaceful people and though very fond of playing at soldiers in their leisure and holiday time yet prefer the growing of dollars during the day . . . .

I should like your daguerrotype portraits. I will pay for them if you will oblige me by getting them done and send them by Mr Moulson or N. Cowlishaw, both of whom are in Sheffield, or will be when this arrives.

There are no botanical gardens here. The ground is so valuable they could not be made to pay. The parks small and scarcely worthy of the name.

I do not dine out and visit little. I might do it to my heart's content if I cared to accept the offers of introductions. The fact is, visiting brings with it numerous expenses which I cannot afford. So I retire content to my room and bury myself with my books. Do not think that I mope; no such thing. I have a few friends and that is all I want. . . . .

Ice water is excellent for keeping up the tone of the stomach. It seems to act as a stimulant.

I have not fished at all but as you say, there is excellent sport. Shooting I might also have if I wished. The woodcock season commences on 4th inst. Quails and partridges also in abundance.

I accepted an invitation into the country to spend the fourth July. I went last Saturday, returned on Tuesday morning about 25 miles by rail, was met at Linnit station by the lady herself, her mother and a friend with a carriage and drove them home, about 6 or 7 miles. Drove carriage and pair to church on Sunday morning and again at night. Was caught in a severe thunderstorm returning. Enjoyed myself very much indeed and may go again whenever I choose.

I opened my box of books only tonight, would not do it till I felt quite settled. With love to each and to all my friends, I remain dear Father and Mother,

Yours dutifully,

Jno S. Webb

No. 10   79 Cranberry St. Brooklyn,   July 23/53

Dear Parents,

You need not be afraid of the boat rowing. I possess too much caution to place my life in jeopardy. It is a very healthy pastime and was strongly recommended to me by Mr Nicholson.

On Tuesday I was obliged to talk to Mr Jno Marsden, late of Westfield Terrace. He sat next to me in a stage. I have hitherto avoided him as he is in bad favour with his countrymen here. I am obliged to be very careful who I associate with as people's characters are severely criticised and they are judged in a great measure by the company they keep. It is a most laughable thing that amongst this republican people there is as much caste as in England itself and yet they pride themselves on the chimerical idea of equality. . . . .

Flies are troublesome at times and I am fain to use a fan now and then, both to cool myself and keep them off. Great quantities of fans made of palm leaf are exported from China and sold here at 3 cents each. Gents may often be seen carrying parasols or umbrellas to keep off the sun and the sunny side of the street is comparatively deserted.

Give my regards to Mr Shim and tell him that the milk here is not so good as his, partly because the grazing in this neighbourhood is poor and partly because of the cupidity of the milk sellers, in making too free with the black cow. The land on which New York stands and the neighbourhood is nothing but a loose sand to a great depth, and though trees flourish grass seems to pine and want nourishment.

I remain your affectionate & dutiful son

Jno. S. Webb

No. 9 GMW   79 Cranberry St. Brooklyn

Augt. 1st 1853

Dear George,*

If I were not a methodical old batchelor [sic] I should not send you a letter this week as you are already five in my debt, but as your name stands next on my list I cannot help it.

I have carried out the plan I proposed about Church attendance. I am now fully installed at St Ann's, as member and teacher & anticipate much more comfort, edification and opportunities of usefulness than as a wanderer. I feel now as if I had a home in God's house, an earnest of a better home above. Dr Butler is a most estimable man, a faithful plainspoken Preacher without either pride or bigotry, desirous above all things to awaken in his hearers a sense of their guilt and of God's mercy, & after bringing them to the foot of the Cross, to build them up in their most holy faith. Sometime ago his church was undergoing extensive repairs which occupied 16 weeks. The Episcopal Methodist Church in Sands St. close by was offered to him for the purpose of assembling his people during that time and gladly accepted. The services commenced at ½ past 8 & 5 so as not to interfere with the others. After a while Sands St. church was

* J.S.W.'s brother Rev. George Mower Webb, Vicar of Aughton

burnt down and he took the opportunity of returning the favour by offering the use of his Church in like manner. Is it not pleasant to see such good feeling amongst Christians? I attended Sacrament last Sunday for the first time in America. There were a great number, between 200 & 300. The afternoon service was postponed till night.

I went up to my friend Sawyer's lodgings after dinner, & not finding him at home, I went along to Miss Perigow's where I found the rogue. He had been taking her to church in the morning and had staid there to dinner. We spent the afternoon together and I accompanied him to his home and took Tea there. At night he & I went to Washington St. Church and heard a very good sermon by Mr Fox of Sands St. Church. Dr Kennedy is from home having gone with his eldest daughter to Saratoga a famous watering place in this state. After service Sawyer introduced me to Misses Jane and Kate Kennedy & more sensible, intelligent & pleasant Ladies I never wish to see. They far eclipse all my other Brooklyn friends. Unfortunately their father's time is almost expired so that we cannot hope to enjoy their society long. Miss Jane is my favourite, her sister is too still. You see I tell you all the gossip. I think I see my grave brother George shake his head & consider what he shall say in his next lecture to that scrapegrace John. Well, go on, give me good advice, and if it accords with my inclinations, I will try to follow it.

Littlewood went down to Newark on Saturday night to spend Sunday with Miss Marshall's who have lately come over from Sheffield. I shall get introduced the first opportunity. After all, female friends are the best a young man can have, & I do not intend to be without. But I have great comfort in my friend Sawyer, he is a noble-minded young man & one worthy both of esteem & respect. He & Littlewood meet in class. I went with them last Wednesday week but do not much like it.

Poor Mrs White is gone at last, and Edley our old neighbour. I never see a Sheffield paper, but I see a record of one or more well-known names being blotted out of the Book of Life. I almost dread to look lest it should tell of any who are near & dear to me. God grant that I meet *you* all again in the flesh in peace & joy. Oh! what a happy meeting it will be if so.

Give my kind regards to all my Aughton relatives and friends and accept the same from

Yr affectionate Brother

J.S. Webb

No.12

Dear Parents,

I am not going to put you off with the scanty note I sent you last week, as that was only an envelope for the letter enclosed to the school. I am waiting for the train to Bridgport, Conn. where I intend going and may perhaps take a short tour in that state. It is one of the disadvantages under which I labour that I have not only the customers themselves to find but also to seek out the various seats of manufacture and commerce. It is for this purpose I am about to travel.

You need not fear the continued rising of prices. There is not going to be any war except perhaps between Turkey and Greece.[*] It is as I expected with Hempsall. If he wishes to come out I advise him to take a situation at first in some dry goods store in New York.

I hope dear M.A.'s recovery though slow will be sure. If the length of the hay harvest causes her protracted suffering it is a pity she is not here. The grass is cut in the morning and led in the evening. But as such a dignified person as the Duke of Devonshire has the same illness, M.A. must consider the great honour of being *anyhow* like his Grace. Hot as the weather is, I like the climate so far better than that of my native land. This is a free country, everyone wears his beard whiskers or not, just as he likes and no-one asks why. I intend having my chin well covered when winter comes, but now it is pleasanter to go without.

I have heard some surprising news this morning, Aug. 15/53 so much so as to be scarcely credible. I am informed that Mr Moss and the two Gambles are joining in partnership and further that Thos. G. is coming out to represent the new firm. I could not help laughing when I remembered a conversation I had with him a short time before I left, when he asserted his desire to stay in the old country. So much for intentions when a man is driven along the sea of circumstances, his bark must go before the breeze, unless he be furnished with the heavy anchors of obstinacy or prejudice. Young Milner, son of Charley Milner, of Fargate, is also crossing . . . I think

[*] March 28/54 Britain & France declared war on Russia, supporting Turkey which had declared war on Russia Oct/53. (Crimea).

England will be coming en masse some day. I took my friend Mondelet on Sunday morning, 7th to Trinity Church, Broadway, N.Y. It is considered a very fine building but is nothing compared to our collegiate churches or cathedrals. He supped with me and accompanied me to Washington St. Church Brooklyn in the evening. I went over to Jersey City next morning to see him off by steamer "Merlin" but found she was not ready, having been delayed two days at the quarantine. We therefore left the luggage aboard and went together at 2½ p.m. by the steam boat down to Coney Island where we very much enjoyed a sea bathe with numbers of others, both ladies and gentlemen. It was my first bathe in the open sea. Each person is provided with a dress on the Island, and the ladies I assure you, look very pretty in their marine bloomer costumes. My friend came home and slept with me. Next day we went to the steamer and I had a very narrow escape of going to Bermuda myself as the gangway was taken in without any notice while I was yet on board. You may think I wasted a deal of time with him but I expect to be recompensed by the friendship so confirmed, both socially and commercially. It is of immense importance to me to extend my acquaintance as much as possible and by this means I hope to make friends not only in Toronto but in Boston and in Montreal.

I had the honour of being introduced to Dr Kennedy, whose name you are already familiar with, as the minister of the Methodist Episcopalian Church in Washington St. Also to his two sons on 9th. They are a very pleasant family and my visits there will be frequent.

What a muss there has been in London about the cabs. Stages run in N.Y. for 3d. a distance of 5 miles but the drivers of the carriages for hire are most dishonest and exorbitant. The heat during the last week has been excessive. I noticed the thermometer in my bedroom on Saturday afternoon at 5 o'clock, the blinds having been down all day, to stand at 94°. At night pleasant breeze sprang up and today it is rather more moderate. The sky gloomy and likely for a thunderstorm. I stand the weather first-rate and now, dear Father and Mother, I will conclude. Keep me *well* posted about all the changes which old Time amuses himself in accomplishing.

I am, dear Parents,

Yours dutifully and affectionately,

Jno. S. Webb

No. 13 P   15 Gold St. New York   Sept 5th '53

Dear Parents,

. . . .

You would not be liable to such vexatious mistakes with your baggage in American Railroads as so frequently occurs in England. You may travel hundreds of miles without seeing it & yet find it all right at the far end. When you take your ticket you get it checked for your destination. A brass ticket with a number is fastened to it & a duplicate is given to you, so that none but yourself can claim it & the Company render themselves liable to a certain amount for its safe restoration.

The Harvest of Wheat, oats, rye & hay, have been already gathered sometime. The wheat is ready here before the hay. The Indian Corn begins to wither, but will not be ripe for a month yet. I read in the newspaper the other day of a stalk 14 feet 7 ins high and a gentleman from the West told me that it was not uncommon for them to be even taller. I have seen plenty myself 12 feet but seven or eight is average. Many fields are now white over with buck wheat. Apples, Pears, Plums, Nectarines are in the Market. Grapes also, but they are scarcely ripe. It is estimated that 60,000 bushels of Peaches are daily brought into N.Y.

I must not forget to thank Father for Lloyd's Newspaper, it was very acceptable & to this date the only one I have received. Who is giving the Mormonite lectures at Ellerton? The Mormons are exerting themselves to the utmost especially in the North of Europe in order to gain a sufficient reputation to be taken into the Union of States.

I was travelling last week in Connecticut & Massachusets. At 4 o'clock on Monday afternoon 29th August I took my passage on board the Granite State Steamer for Hartford Connt. – was much gratified in finding that Mr Chas Pearce Junr. was one of my fellow travellers most of the way & in his company passed a most pleasant evening. The sunset on the Sound is a most glorious sight repaying in itself the whole trouble of the voyage. The colours are most gorgeous, surpassing fancy, and far too bright for any artist to risk on canvas except he cared nothing for ridicule. When afterwards it died away, the Comet * appeared with a splendid galaxy of

---

* not Halley's comet in 1853

47

stars & the phosphorescent lights of the ocean vieing with them in brilliancy. Hertford is much further by boat (175 miles) than rail (112 miles) but it was only a choice between sleeping on board or at an Hotel & I can sleep equally sound in either place. Besides there is more liberty on the boat than in the carriage. You can sit or stand or promenade, talk, read or whistle as you like. A comfortable supper with plenty of time to eat it, instead of the hasty snack standing with the almost immediate summons "all aboard", besides missing all the dust with which you get covered on the road, and it is cheaper.

But must conclude,

Yours dutifully,

Jno. S. Webb

MA 11 (this is the first letter extant written to his elder sister, Mary Ann (Polly)

15 Gold St. New York   Sept. 6th '53

Dear Mary Ann,

At the time I left off with my letter to our parents I was star-gazing on board the "Granite State" steamer in the Sound on my way to Hartford. Well, after eating the greater part of a mush melon, to quench my real or fictitious thirst, I turned into my berth and woke a little before 5 o'clock Tuesday morning. I arose and dressed and as the steamer had stopped, fully expected I had arrived. I was disappointed on finding that we had only just entered the Connecticut River and were waiting at a country landing place called Middle Haddam for a thick fog to clear away. By and Bye the sun asserted his supremacy and we proceeded. We stopped again to land goods and passengers at Middletown, about 15 miles from Hartford, and while there a man deliberately walked down to the dock and jumped into the river to drown himself. This he did with such indifference and nonchalance that though I saw the whole proceeding as I stood on the forward deck, not 30 yards off, his purpose never occurred to my mind till his wife came running down wringing her hands and looking the image of despair. There were numbers of people about as you suppose, and they first attempted to get him out with pieces of plank but he would not take hold, then one of them jumped in and taking hold with one hand held up the other to his comrades to pull at, but that did not succeed as the landing place was high. A boat with 3 men now came out and soon got him in, but while engaged with their oars, the determined suicide gave them the slip, and managed, though he was partially incapacitated, to roll over into the water. He was soon taken in, however, and they kept him fast till they got to land. I have not heard since what became of him. Both he and his wife appeared to be Irish of the labouring class. This was about 8 AM and at 10 o'clock we got to Hartford after being 18 hours on the way, whereas by rails we could reach it in 4½ hours. I dined at the American Hotel and having finished business there, went forward to Springfield, 26 miles, by the ¼ to 5 PM train, and arriving about 6 put up at the City Hotel. I must tell you that at Hartford I saw the famous Charter Oak, the tree in which the charter of independence was hid at a time of peculiar danger during the revolutionary war. It is a venerable tree, and the acorns, which get fewer every year, are considered as relics, and the cups frequently made into fancy pincushions. Its hollow trunk is defended from the weather by patches of zinc or lead and the hole itself, which served the patrols in their time of necessity has an iron door fixed into it and locked up!

At night (Tuesday) I committed an act of indiscretion by eating too much pineapple just before getting into bed and suffered sickness the next day in consequence. I thought then that Mother's little slice was the better share. On Wednesday night ¼ to 7 I started for Chicopee Falls, 5½ miles, a village of factories. Here are immense cotton factories and the Ames Man(n)ing Co. carry on an extensive business in cannon, guns, swords and all other implements of war. I put up at the Factory Hotel, a real country establishment, I put my shoes outside the door but found them in the same dusty condition the next morning. There was no mirror in my chamber so I had to shave by guess. Breakfast ½ p 6 but I did not get to it till ½ p 7. Started at 9 AM for Cabot, a similar place two miles distant, dined at Cabot House and off to Holyoke, ¼ to 2 PM, 5 miles. This is a growing place of factories and what was more interesting to me, a large machine shop employing 600 hands. A first rate Hotel was built here some time since, but its time is not yet come. It is at present closed. In this place I was obliged to buy a pair of shoes as I was completely and litterally [sic] run aground. The American leather is no better than paper.

From here I proceeded to Meriden at ¾ to 4 PM, 52 miles, or rather I wished to do so but could get no further than Springfield, 8 miles, where I staid to sup at the American Hotel and started by the first train at ½ p 7 arrived in Meriden at 8.55 PM. What was my consternation to find on enquiry that all the rooms in the Hotel were taken, but I was soon relieved by hearing that at the top of the hill there was another. Fortunately one of my fellow passengers was in the same case and accompanied me or I might have sought long enough for the top of the hill in the dark. After walking ½ mile or so we came to another real country specimen, dignified with the name of the Central Hotel, where, however, I passed a very comfortable night, though at breakfast I could not eat the piece of buttered leather they called steak. At noon I went by stage to Waterbury 14 miles ¼ past 1. It was excessively hot, 8 of us packed inside, the sun too busy roasting to make the outside berth much pleasanter than torture by slow fire. We were 2¾ hours on the road which was very hilly. This is the character of the State, many of the rocks rise steep and precipitous as the lover's leap in Middleton Vale[*] and being clothed with trees to the very summit looked grand and imposing. To add to our unpleasant situation, some of the ladies said they were always sick inside a coach so that every moment I expected to have ocular demonstration of a most unpleasant nature and considered how I could best save my pants. Arrived at Waterbury I put up at Scovill House, a most comfortable hotel, made the best use of the remainder of the day and after supper dropped in at a covenant meeting in the Baptist Chapel. Next morning, finding myself short of time, I took a carriage and finishing my calls went down to the station and off I went to Ansonia, 14 miles at ¼ to 9 AM, dined there at Perkins Hotel and off to Derby at ¼ to 2, two miles. It consists of a few villa residences, shops, &c, but close to it at the other side of the Naugatuck River is a thriving manufacturing town which they have named Birmingham – ambitious perhaps but some day it may rival its distinguished prototype.

While waiting for the train I weighed myself at the station. The result shewed 127½ lbs, 3½ lbs higher than when I left England. This, I think, is very good considering the heat and I may look forward to gaining

[*] near Sheffield, England.

considerably in the winter. I started for New York 72 miles at $\frac{1}{4}$ to 2 PM where I arrived about $\frac{1}{4}$ to 8 PM and at *home* about 9. Mr Cottier would prepare me a supper and acted as a second mother and I was glad that for a short time my wanderings were over.

I have not dared to describe each place as my limits would not allow, but I may observe that for the most part they are picturesque and new, having sprung up like mushrooms, the buildings good, some fine, and being interspersed with trees they preserve a country appearance. Waterbury is a remarkable instance. A few years since, a mere village, it now contains 7,000 inhabitants, has lately been made a city and bids fair for the future. The whole distance of my week's journey was only $367\frac{1}{2}$ miles, a mere step.

For Sunday I have a very bad account to give. I was again too late for school and therefore prepared staying away from St Ann's. I and Littlewood went over in the morning to New York, to hear the Rev. *Mrs* Brown preach in the Metropolitan Hall. Her text was "Do not this abominable thing which I hate" – from Jeremiah. Her attacks, or remarks, I ought to say, were directed against what may be called polite or fashionable vices as scandal, wine etc. Her sermon was long and able and was listened to with great attention. She is the minister of a church somewhere in the north west of New York State. I saw two bloomers on my way there and met them again returning. In my eyes they looked very pretty. The ladies are having high times in the City holding temperance and women's rights conventions.

Yesterday I left my office at 5 o'clock to remove to my new lodgings in Clinton St. and though I felt some regret at leaving Cottier's yet when I got my things fixed in my snug room I did not in the least repent my determination. There was a great source of annoyance, I did not mention, and that was the younger children who were most unruly and not at all in subjection to their fond parents. I am now as snug as batchelorism will permit of but I find I must defer a description of my new home for want of space.

I remain, dear Mary Ann, with much love

Your affectionate brother,

Jno. S. Webb

No. 11 GMW   Franklin House

                    Lawrence Masstts   Sept. 10th '53

Dear George,

I received yours of 24th Augt. this morning in Boston, it having been forwarded from New York.

You must not get proud now you have a carriage. Literally it will not exalt you much. I shall like to hear of your success with the library. You cannot do better than promote reading amongst your people provided they are supplied with suitable books. You should by all means be acquainted with every book in the library so that in your visits they might form the ground for interesting conversation & serve as vehicles for further instruction.

On Wednesday afternoon at 5 o'clock I left in the Empire State Steamer for Boston accompanied by friend Littlewood who had also business there. Though at the outset the clouds were heavy and threatening yet we had a most pleasant night, got to the Fall River at $\frac{1}{2}$ past 5 Tuesday morning & took the rail forward to Boston where we arrived at 8 though it was near 9 before we got to Revere House with having to wait our turn for the luggage.

I was pegging away at business at Boston till Saturday noon I should not have got through in a week if I had not hired a carriage which was also necessary on account of the heavy samples I carried. Saturday noon I drove out to Roxbury, an out township about $2\frac{1}{2}$ miles distant, and having settled at the Hotel before I started and taken the luggage in the gig, I drove straight to the Boston & Main R.R. depot on my return and Littlewood who accompanied me & saved me the expense of a footman to take care of the horse while I made my calls, took the gig home. I find a considerable advantage in getting into a strange place the night before, for though too late for business, I have time to look round, enquire, & make my plans and lists for next day. Littlewood tried to persuade me to stay Sunday with him in Boston where he will not finish till Monday night, but beside the reason I gave you, it is so expensive there, I did not feel comfortable to do so. Boston is called the Tremonte or Trimount city from being built on three hills. It has a more English appearance than any place I have yet seen except Montreal. I have two more Customers to see here who are out of town but expected home this morning. Lawrence is the most remarkable mushroom city I know. It only dates its commencement from 1848 & now contains a population of 15,000. The establishment of two large cotton Mills, one giving employment to 2,300 hands, and the other 1,700, also a machine shop of 700 hands are the principal causes of its advancement. It covers a good deal of ground, but as a man said, to whom I was conversing on the subject, it wants filling up. There are about 10 churches comprising Episcopal, Unitarian, Congregational, Universalists, Baptists, Freewill Baptists, Roman Caths. Metht. Epl. but the most singular are the second advent Christians. They preach and many devoutly believe that our Saviour's coming will be next year.They have been disappointed more than once, the last time was in 1848. Some have gone so far as to give up all their goods, & if I may judge from the manner of their Preacher (to whom I listened on the stairs for a few minutes) his object is to excite them as much as possible. Whether it is sincerity or a pious fraud to make People more earnest in seeking Salvation, or a gross imposition to extort money, or a device of Satan to cause them to throw off religion altogether, when the time of blasted hopes, and disappointed expectations arrives; I cannot say but this I know, it is not of God for it is contrary to his word.

Yesterday I went in the afternoon to the congregational & in the evening was going to Mother ch. but met the people coming out, though it was only 7 o'clock. The hours of Service vary so much in different places that it is impossible to guess right. There are no Presbyterians here & but few through the New England States, though so numerous in the South. But I must hasten to conclude that I may finish and go forward. The weather is getting much cooler. The Thermometer in the Hotel ranges yesterday & today between 52° and 62°. Quite frosty air this morning when I rose.

With love to each & all,

I remain dear George,

Yrs truly

Jno S. Webb

Providence, Rhode Island   Sept. 19th '53

Dear Mary Ann,

I received your letter of 25th August at Boston on 10th along with the rest. I like to hear from you but your letters grieve me at the same time that they give me pleasure. Why do you not allow me a brother's privilege of assisting you without making such a fuss about it? It only reminds me of what I want to forget, and that is the smallness of my contribution; fain would I increase it if it were only in my power, but I feel now more sure of success. I have made an impression on this journey which I hope will be seen and felt before long . . . .

Taunton Tuesday afternoon ½ p 4. I came here by the 11 o'clock train this morning and early as it is I have nothing left to do. I have made all my calls here and if it were not for some appointments for morning I should have left for Fall River tonight. This leisure I use to finish my letter to you. The distance between Providence and Taunton by rails is 30 miles for which I paid only 50c. or not 1d. a mile. The usual rate on most of the American lines except where there is competition is nearly 3c. or about 2½d.

Tell Rose that though I do not wear her purse, it is not because I have no regard for the maker and bestower. The fact is most of the American money is in paper, from 1 dollar notes upwards; gold is comparatively little used and silver very scarce. On this account I find a port monie[*] more convenient – and purses are rarely seen.

You silly thing to be frightened at the rain. I read in the papers that the storm we had at Lowell the night previous to the firemen's competition did much damage in New York and Brooklyn, amongst other freaks blowing down a magnificent willow in Clinton St. but some distance from my lodgings. I hope to be there on Thursday. This journey has taken a longer time than (my visit to) Canada, though the distance will be something under 700 miles.

I herewith send a little map to give you a better idea of the situation of each place.

[*] wallet

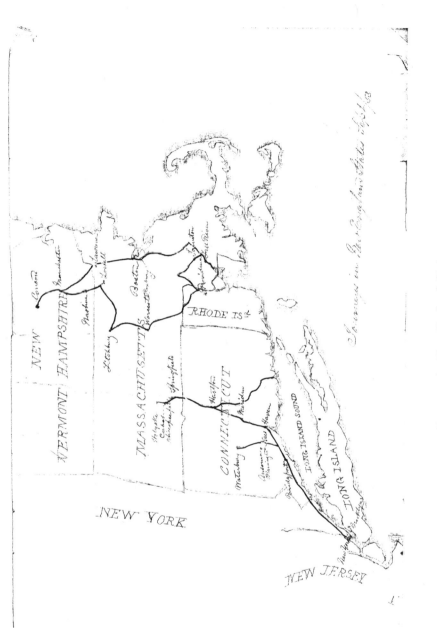

Journeys in New England States

There is no better way of learning geography than by travelling and by having the opportunity of seeing and obtaining information on the spot. I am getting better posted up about the country, its productions, capabilities and progress than the natives themselves. Vegetation is now changing its colours. The Indian Corn is withered and the ears ripening fast. The buckwheat which covered the fields a while ago with its white blossoms is in many places cut down and fixed up into ruddy ricks to harvest. The vine of the squash has dwindled almost out of sight, leaving the round yellow fruit to strew the ground as if a quantity of immense oranges had been scattered over it. While speaking of it I may tell you that it makes a most delicious vegetable and an equally good pie. In the former state it has the appearance of mashed swede turnips and in the latter of custard, or rather cheese-cake. Grapes are ripe, and that splendid fruit the American apple (which is, you know, imported largely into England) is now in its prime. The sweet potatoe is not one of the worst vegetables of this land, and my palate is becoming so Yankified that it may ultimately obtain the preference with me over the old fashioned murphy. Peaches are still in high favour though they are neither so large nor so sweet in these parts as down below New York.

The land all through the parts I have been the last fortnight is nothing but sand and stone, abounding in brushwood and small trees and covered in many places with a small yellow flowering weed which itself indicates the poverty of the soil. The trees are just beginning to change their colour and some have already assumed the rich autumnal tints. I look forward to a pleasant time which is called the Indian Summer[*] and takes place usually about now or a little later. Then comes the nipping time when you must run to get out of Tom Frost's way, he is so eager to get hold of you or else wrap up in such a way that his fingers will not freeze you.

I met with one of those extraordinary fanatics called second advent christians, and found that in their creed they deny the immortality of the soul, affirm that it dies with the body and is re-animated with it at the resurrection. They hold that at the judgement day when the righteous will be admitted into life eternal the wicked will be annihilated, for that

[*] now a commonplace in England

56

is the construction they put upon everlasting death. They are looking forward to the immediate or approximate coming of Jesus Christ. Never before did I feel so much the necessity of being able to give a reason of the faith and hope which is in me, for this man was evidently sincere and brought chapter and verse to prove his affirmations. I laughed at the sect when I first heard of them and wondered they could be so foolish to give themselves up to such foolish notions but now I find I must search more deeply if I would lend a helping hand to uproot this heresy.

I will now go to bed and try to dream about you though to tell the truth I do not think I shall and as for the bed I never enjoy it. I sleep so soundly. Goodnight darling I am yours

Jno S. Webb.

No. 14 P

Earls Hotel,
Providence Rhode Island
Sept 19 '53

Dear Parents,

As with Travellers across the Mountains 'Hills rise o'er hills', so it is with me town after town; City after City presents itself, urging its claim to a visit till I verily believe without staying long in any place, I might be continually agoing, like the Wandering Jew or the Maid with the Cork Leg; when I started from N.Y. I did not intend to be absent more than a week. I now see no prospect of getting back next Wednesday or Thursday; there is an ample field of labor in the New England States, & I am of opinion the Yankees possess a more energetic & enterprising Character than their Southern neighbours.

I left Concord last Tuesday afternoon at ½ past 4 for Nashua distant 35 miles towards Boston, passing through Manchester arrived at the station, I looked about for the City & could see none. I had to ask where is Nashua. But seeing some Hotel Carriages I took my seat in one of them thinking it might realise my wish better than even the famous Magic Mirror, was driven up to the Pearl St. House a very good Hotel. At Night I strolled about the place as I make a point of doing to learn the ins and outs like a Cat or a Rabbit making acquaintance with its next residence. I was attracted by a church Bell, & learning it summoned to a church meeting of the Congregationalists I went in also, not able to resist the kind invitation of a young Lady of whom I made the enquiry. In the Minister I saw a second Mr Smith of St Mary's, just his manner, method, & earnestness, & was much pleased & edified.

I left Nashua on Wednesday & proceeded to Lowell still nearer Boston & exactly the same distance from it as Lawrence but on a more westerly route. It is an extensive manufacturing city comprising very large cotton & woollen factories, machine works etc. The operatives at Lowell are in admirable order & condition the result of the wise & excellent regulations adopted by the Factory Corporations. Lowell contains a population estimated at 37,000. The boarding houses for the factory hands are built with every convenience and modern improvement & being owned by the Corporation themselves are let only to people of unimpeachable character who are bound to observe certain rules & on no account to take in any boarders but those connected with the factories. The consequence of all this is that there is no hesitation to work in such places on the ground of low or demoralizing association and more efficient & respectable people are ready to accept employment than is usually the case. The day after my arrival there was a competition amongst many of the fire companies of this and the neighbouring States. About 26 Companies each in different uniforms, attended by 16 bands of musicians including upwards of 1600 men, paraded the City in the forenoon with the Fire Engines & hose Carriages tastefully ornamented with flowers & evergreens, one drawn by 42 men, another by 6 beautiful grey horses, others by both horses & men. Seated in front of one were three little boys fancifully dressed in old fashioned styles & a large handsome Newfoundland dog, apt emblem of succour from a devouring element. The chief engineers were on horseback & acted as marshalls of procession. It was a most stirring sight and you need not wonder that all Lowell were at their heels. The Night had been very wet & the morning commenced with a drizzly rain but soon after Nine it cleared up & the afternoon was bright & pleasant as could be wished. After dinner they formed again & marched to the place appointed, where was fixed a very tall Pole by which the power of each engine might be tested. So anxious were they to succeed that some burst their hose, others forced it off the engine and got drenched with water. A piece of high ground & a Copse rose just behind, reminding me of the hill & wood in the Botanical

58

Gardens at home on a grand public day covered with people. It was such a sight as you would never see in England, though as the need of fire Engines is less you have not reason to regret it.

I left Lowell for Fitchburg (52 miles) to the West, a small place of not more than 3-4000 inhabitants, put up at the American Hotel, a very good House and notwithstanding the scenery all along is very grand, the country is wild & uncultivated & very hilly. Fitchburg is situated in a narrow valley with the hills rising high on each side.

On Friday left at 12.40 for Worcester 26 miles to the South, an old established City of some 20,000. Agricultural implements Machinery tools and pistols are amongst the chief productions there. I staid at the American Temperance Hotel. Worcester, I think the prettiest place I have yet seen as regards its situation & I was almost sorry to be obliged to leave it so soon. I started for Providence on Saturday at 4.10 pm. (43 miles) to the S.E. where I am at present located and from the size of the place I judge, shall not be ready to leave before Friday night. It contains 17,000 inhabitants & has some claim to antiquity. I was tempted here by some large locomotive works, and hope to do some trade before I leave. There are many other places I should like to go to but unless I hear of something too good to miss I shall proceed direct from here to New London & take Steam Boat for New York. I have heaps of places to see before Xmas & must give each a turn.

Providence Monday night

Yesterday morning I walked out after breakfast & mounting one of the hilly streets had a first-rate view of the City. It is a charming place & what is most remarkable both in this, & most other towns or Cities carrying an extensive Manufactures, there is none of that smoke or dirt so common to similar places in England. This as I have before times observed is the consequence of the use of Anthracite instead of Bituminous coal. It burns more like Coke – bright & hot.

As the morning was drizzly I poked my Nose into a Sunday School and took a class to keep me out of Mischief, and afterwards attended the Church St John's (Episl). Here I found that the successor's to the Apostles, who preached to us, was not quite so exclusive as his English Brethren. For he gave out notice that in the evening an address would be given in The Central Congregational Church by Doctor Tully on behalf of the persecuted protestants of Madeira. I went to hear him & was much interested in his account of the sufferings he himself had undergone & the Cruelties inflicted on his converts. Some 500 have already taken refuge in Illinois but there still remains some 200. They are very poor. The potatoe rot & disease amongst the Grapes have together caused a famine & nothing better is anticipated for the next year so that they have no power to help each other. They wish to flee from their persecutors & join their brethren for which purpose $6000 would be required. For worshipping God in their scriptural way or trying to make converts or reading the Bible they are liable to 3 yrs imprisonment, & five men who would not attend mass there were locked up into a most loathsome dungeon full of vermin where was only just room to lie down. Their judges are Priests so there can be little chance of mercy.

I must now conclude with unlimited love to my dear parents.

I remain as ever
Yrs, J.S. Webb

No. 12 GMW

From Miss Thompson's
18 Clinton St. Brooklyn
Sept. 29th '53

Dear George,

. . . .

After the excitement & bustle of travelling I confess that home feels a little lonesome, the more so as my friends Littlewood & Sawyer (I mention these names so often that it will be like the old tale of the Browns & the Brittlebanks, of my father's youthful days) went on a visit to our friend at Wayneflete, and did not return till Wednesday morning. On Saturday night to keep off the blues, I sallied out to visit a young lady Miss Read, and succeeded in passing an hour or two in agreeable conversation. My evenings have since been occupied in reading a very excellent book, Success in Life, by a Scotch author. It is arranged in chapters under different heads, such as Integrity, Decision, Economy, Courtesy, Benevolence &c. illustrated by biographical extracts. Of Lord Eldon it remarks that his indecision which caused the Court of Chancery to become a byeword arose from the following circumstance.

"On his leaving school for Oxford he travelled from Newcastle to London in a fly which was a remarkably quick kind of coach for those days, though it took 3 or 4 days & nights for the journey. On the door panel he observed the motto *Sat cito si sat bene* * & was ever influenced in after life by the sentiment." My motto is 'Go ahead' but I will be careful not to make more haste than 'good speed', and when I am opposed or hindered in my exertions, instead of fretting & fuming at slow progress, I will say to myself *Sat cito si sat bene.*

On Sunday night I heard Dr Kennedy at Washington St. I may possibly join that church for there the seats are free, a Collection being taken up during the service, at which only one or two Cents are expected. I was quite dismayed at being told the price of a sitting at St Ann's $10 or 2 guineas sterling. This is more than I can afford & more than I feel willing to give.

On Monday afternoon I went up to the Crystal Palace not having been for a month before. I found it in a state of greater completeness. The Picture gallery & the Machinery department are thrown open & form interesting features in the exhibition. In the former is a picture which shows the true national feeling. It is called "Diogenes successful" & represents that eccentric earthworm casting the light of his lantern on Washington who stands as if haranguing & pointing to the alter of Liberty on which he has placed the Constitution, watched over & protected by the American Eagle which hovers above. There are many Pictures of merit but I will not dwell on the subject now.

I intend during Winter frequently to go at night & examine things critically when possibly, if acceptable, I may give you the result of my observations. Among the things which cannot fail to attract the wandering gaze is a Velocipede of very simple construction in which a Man is patiently and perseveringly riding about in order to show its advantages. Also Machines of various kinds weaving various textures & fabrics with marvelous precision & speed. That we are not in such a place as the British Museum & that the Spectacle is to serve a more selfish end than to please & instruct beholders, or promote peace & unity among the

---

* quickly (or soon) enough if well enough

61

nations, is sufficiently evident from the quantity of Circulars & Cards here & there, & in some cases a book, on which is written "Any Orders put down here will be punctually attended to". This is the Lever which moves the World.

Sept. 30th By the Washington Steamer just arrived from Europe we have News of Importance concerning Russia. The refusal of the Czar to the terms submitted by the allied powers, & the probability of a war which may affect the whole of the continent. We are all looking anxiously for the "American Steamer" which will bring News 3 days later. It is a thousand pities that the Bear is so true to its Nature. Commerce will languish; many lives will be sacrificed, & much misery caused thereby to the survivors, & last but not least, the permanent establishment of Peace by Arbitration put off to an indefinite period.

How do you succeed with your Parish Library school &c. Miss Valentine has not sent me the sketch of Bubwith Church. Tell her I shall prize it very much. Oh! how I long to see the old places & faces again. I think if ever the time arrives for a visit, I shall go mad with joy, & yet I could not easily settle down in the old ways again, but should want to be back here. What a discontented fickle thing is Man and I of all Men the most.

I have been told that Mr Moss is coming out to establish a trade for the new firm Moss & Gambles. I have a famous opportunity now for improving my mind in the solitude & silence of long Nights. But do not on this account expect to find in me a paragon or fountain of learning. You know why. "Infirm of purpose; hasty to resolve" etc. has been most applicable to my case, but I will indulge in no vain regrets, but resolve & re-resolve to mend my ways, & to redeem my time in these my later days.

I am dear George still your affe. brother

Jno S. Webb

No. 15   18 Clinton St. Brooklyn   Oct 4th '53

Dear Parents,

. . . .

The foreign news is particularly interesting just at this time when peace or war affecting all Europe hangs on the lips of one man. The papers are read most eagerly as soon as they arrive and the American press teems with remarks, commendations and animadversions on the conduct of the various governments and diplomatists implicated. Of course, there is a great deal which my English stomach will not* swallow but there is much which tends to remove national and party prejudices and form broader and more liberal opinions. I do not say that I am a democrat but I am no Tory.

After service we went to Cooke's where besides other things we were regaled on grapes grown behind the house and that is situated in a throng part of the city. They taste very different to ours, are pulpy instead of juicy, are sucked out of their skins and then swallowed whole, stones & all.

. . . .

The winter season is coming on, and I expect to participate in some of the evening classes, but I fear they will be stiff affairs compared with many I have taken part in at home.

. . . .

I did not read about the ladies liking ice cream, nor had I any need to do so. I know if from experience.

. . . . I get my papers now that they are stamped. I thank Father for the "News of the World".

I expect Mr Moss by the "Arabia" which arrived yesterday and even went up to the Astor House to see if he were there, but have since been informed that he was not amongst her passengers. His father's sudden death at Buxton has no doubt been the cause of the delay. I have not therefore received the letters which he bears for me. Amongst the recent importations from Sheffield I may mention Mr Pycock and Mr Rowarth. They both came out in the "Africa". The former is acquainted with Mr Sawyer. My surprise was great when on coming down to tea on Wednesday I saw him seated at the table with his round jolly face.

. . . . I wish Mr Sandford would follow his friend's example, he would perhaps get rid of some of his missnancy ways which are even discernible in his letter. I thank him for it, and was very proud to be remembered. Mother was the first person I have heard quote scripture to justify curtain lectures. When you speak of the female lecturers do not

---

* a classic mixed metaphor! TBD.

confound them with the bulk of American women who look upon them with disgust. The American institutions are however, favourable in their development by the power they give married women to hold and even acquire property independent of the husband. I am sorry Father ran after Moulson and Cowlishaw so much. A few months in America would teach him to set a proper value on himself.

I remain, dear parents,

yours dutifully,

Jno S. Webb.

No. 13 GMW   18 Clinton St.   Oct 13th 1853

Dear George,

. . . .

Harmer appears to be glad to be in New York again. San Francisco is a fine City, has an agreeable climate but Society is scarce and everything very dear. A brown felt low crowned hat cost him $20 which I suppose might be had for one in Sheffield. New York is an expensive place to live in. I gave $4 for a black hat the other day & a pair of boots I have ordered will, I suppose, cost $5¾. I brought boots from England and a good hat too but cannot wear them without making myself a laughing stock. Clothes I must get from home for they are an awful price. Nothing has happened to me very remarkable. Last Wednesday I was at Paterson, same day I had my daguiretype [sic] taken which I intend sending home by the next chance. Friday night I was busy *fixing* my Accordion which I had rather got out of order.

. . . .

You are right in your remarks on the cheapness of Books, the two principal reasons are, no tax on paper & the bookseller being at Liberty to sell at his own price & not the publisher's. For instance Harper's Magazine a work equal to most of our periodicals, is published at 25 cents but sold at many bookshops for 15 cents or 7½d. Blackwoods in England sold for 2/6d, reprinted here at 25 cents or 1/-d, being pirated it cannot pass the English Customs House. I intended writing you another page but must now conclude.

With love,

Yours J. S. Webb

Daguerrotype of J.S. Webb at Paterson NJ USA 1853

No. 16   18 Clinton St. Brooklyn   Oct. 27th/53

Dear Parents,

Your, that is Mother's letter, of 6th came to hand on 19th. You may see by the above address an answer to your question. I am still at home though not contentedly so. I have been obliged to wait the arrival of some goods, which I am anxious to send out before I start. The vessel is now unloading and unless something else occurs to prevent me, I shall be on the wing shortly. I have spent a good deal of the last week at the Custom House, which I assure you is an excellent market for patience and am doing but little at home as the opportunities are very limited. Our weather lately has been wintry, Monday in particular was uncomfortable, raining hard the whole day; it felt so raw that I was obliged to begin with a fire both in my room and office. You should only see how snug I am. All I want is a cheerful face and a kindly greeting, someone I can "tell my mind to" as

Polly would say. A homely face to sit at the table while I read and when tired of that to speak to and sympathise with, to relate the doings and experience of the day and prepare one for the encounters of the next. But as this *is not* I must be content with my silent friends and guess I shall become a regular book-worm. I have lately been engrossed with "Queechy" a book which Susan has no doubt mentioned to you, but it raises a wish which can never be realised of possessing myself of a "Fleda" so pure, so loving, so discreet to be my good angel, my Elfie. What a pity that authors make their characters all perfection, and cause their readers to be discontented with realities. Such an one would indeed fulfill the rights of women –

> The right to wake where others sleep,
> The right to watch, the right to weep,
> The right to comfort in distress,
> The right to soothe, the right to bless,
> The right the widow's heart to cheer,
> The right to dry the orphan's tear,
> The right to feed and clothe the poor,
> The right to teach them to endure,
> The right when other friends have flown
> And left the sufferer all alone,
> To kneel a dying couch beside,
> And meekly point to him who died,
> The right a happy home to make
> In any clime for Jesus' sake
> Rights such as these are all we crave
> Until we ask a quiet grave.

I have now in hand a voluminous history of the United States, being determined to be well acquainted with the country of my adoption. Do not fear my getting through the winter. If I must, I must. Mr Moss will be here on Friday. The steamer "Niagara" in which he is coming arrived at Halifax at 1 o'clock this morning.

. . . .

One of our townsmen has got himself into trouble. Dr W.C. Moss' son, the Moss who kept the druggist's shop on Hale's Moor. He was returning to his lodgings about 1 o'clock Sunday morning with a friend when he met three men and said something which provoked them, on which a skeefle [sic] ensued in which Moss drew a dirk and stabbed one of the men dead. The inquest was held yesterday and is adjourned till Monday. This happened in Degraw St., Brooklyn.

Sawyer is down in Philadelphia. We have seen little of one another since I came to the house, having our separate engagements. I will not write more now as I may want to put in a postscript before I send off.

I am, dear Parents, as ever your most affectionately

Jno S. Webb

Nov. 2nd P.S.

Is Carpenter still in the iron wire trade? If so, will father write him for prices and terms, and if not, do you know anyone who is. Some good old house preferred. There was a fire in Gold St. last night at No. 12 Haslam & Co of Sheffield, nearly opposite my office. I happened to be coming past at the time and felt no little anxiety about it as the street is very narrow and the flames were fierce. With some difficulty it was mastered but not till it had gutted the store. There was a bad fire in Fulton St. the other day and several men got burned in the ruins.

I am very comfortable at home with my cosy fire for which I have to pay 50 cents per week. Coal is very dear. But the anthracite coal is very lasting. The fire is fixed ready for lighting. I have only to do that when I get home and put up the blower and the result is a good fire in a few minutes and a rise of 20 degrees or more in the temperature. I left it at about 7 last night and when I returned at $\frac{1}{4}$ to 12 after seeing the fire in N.Y. I found a very snug fire at home.

No. 17   Nov. 18th 1853 Donegana Hotel, Montreal, Ca.

Dear Father and Mother,

Here I am at last and being again on British ground brings me, as it were, nearer home. Father's letter of 15th Sept. did not reach me till 2nd November from the delay in Mr Moss's proposed voyage. In newspaper phrase I may say "Dispatches of a later date have been already received"...............

67

We arrived at Albany about 9 p.m. and I put up at the City Hotel. I finished in Albany by Tuesday noon and off I went by stage to Troy (6 miles) put up at Troy House, was throng all afternoon and at night went up to Mr Quiggen's and supped there. On my return to the hotel I met Mr Cowlishaw there who had called en route for Montreal. On Wednesday morning we went off together at 7.20 a.m. to Montreal, by rails to Whitehall, 73 miles, up Lake Champlain in steamboat, 100 miles, to Plattsburg, and forward to Montreal, 62 miles, which we reached about 11 p.m. I had some coaxing of the excise officer to pass my baggage. He made such objection on account of my patterns.[*]

The scenery up the lake is very fine and must be splendid in summer. It is very narrow. The Hudson itself will vie with it most of its length. The country through which I passed is the scene in which Cooper laid his interesting work "The Last of the Mohicans". On the lake we stopped at a place called Burlington which was the residence of the Rev. Mr Caughey. I heard a little of his proceedings since leaving England. He is still travelling about. The Troy Conference to which he formerly belonged turned him out for staying beyond his time in defiance of them. The New York Conference would have found him a church but he would not be so tied. The Toronto conference has given him a title to preach by making him what they call a located minister, which means just the reverse. He preached in Hamilton for several months with most surprising results. When he commenced the people were cold and heartless and appeared as if nothing would excite them, yet in a short time, three services on Sunday and one every night were attended by crowds of anxious listeners. One man, the principal hotelkeeper, who had been careless, sold out of his hotel and turned preacher. I may possibly meet with Caughey before I leave the North.

On Thursday I was busy in Montreal. It began to snow when I started but came down softly. The weather mild. At night one of the hardware storekeepers called up at the hotel. I expected several but as the snow was thawing they preferred to stay at home.

This morning on entering the breakfast room I was surprised to see Mr Moss. He is gone tonight to Quebec. The streets are all in a slop with

[*] cast iron!

the thaw. I am well prepared for the weather. I have that great heavy cape which I find first rate for travelling. I brought also flannel drawers and shirts, a red nightgown and woollen socks. By the bye, I have found them very useful and wish I had bought more, but with all my extras I am not so muffled as the Canadians themselves with their great fur caps and coats and top boots. It does me good to see how bravely the ladies face the weather so different to the finikin New Yorkers and more like my own dear country women. But anyone who admires a fine turned ankle will be disappointed. Such thick stumps caused by thick woollen stockings and which they do not care to conceal. An attempt was made at sleighing on Friday but there was as much mud as snow. On Saturday the roads were still worse so that I should have been content with a little more coal. On Saturday night I came to Quebec by steamer "John Munn", distance 180 miles. We set off at 6 and arrived here at 1/4 past 6 on Sunday morning. There were several officers on board, two of them were generals but being a *New Yorker*, I of course looked upon them with *contempt*. I am writing this page at the Russell Hotel, But Hark! there is the gong for dinner. It is only 3 p.m. but we are having an early dinner for those who are going by the boat. The usual time is 6 p.m.

Well I have dined on partridge, turkey & plum pudding, not bad fare but I do not spare knife and fork or anxiety would wear me to a skeleton. But I was going to tell you, before that horrid noise disturbed me, that I am writing this in the little parlour of the hotel with a nice blazing fire of Liverpool coal in the grate. And everything so English-like that I can imagine myself in England. Quebec is an antique and unique place, not another city here to compare with it, as for instance its being formed of houses built on the side of a river inhabited by men, women, &c, &c. I regret that neither coming nor going I have any opportunity of seeing the river scenery on account of the darkness. Yesterday morning I sallied out after breakfast and going to the higher parts, I had a bird's eye view of the Lower Town. The houses far below, yet directly under, the narrow streets and people looking as small as rats, the river and shipping, the island of Orleans dividing the stream, the mainland opposite to the left, the parliament house a very handsome pile; all these and a thousand other points of interest would have kept me a considerable time, had it not been for the wind which, cold and strong, drove me to more sheltered quarters. I attended a service in the English Cathedral by which you must not understand a grand edifice like York Minster but a large building in the plainest Norman surmounted by a low steeple. The interior is fitted up in the old style high pews, contains a very fine organ and arched diamond roof. The singing was excellent, the sermon same style as the building. In the afternoon I went to the Wesleyan Chapel and came in for a prayer meeting. This is a pretty gothic building. At night I went to the Scotch church. In all these places I was pleased to join in our dear old tunes, all my favourites, they might have sung them for my pleasure. The Romanists are very numerous and their cathedral is a fine one. But they are just going off to the boat, so must finish another time. Farewell, Quebec.

Tuesday afternoon 22nd 20 minutes past 2.

Here I am again at Donegana's Hotel. We have had a long passage here and did not get in till ½ past 12. The navigation of the river is difficult in the dark. Last night there was a haze which obliged them to stop and let off their steam. The current is strong and going upstream takes a longer time than coming down. The time however passed pleasantly in conversation about moose, deer, trout fishing and the Indians. It is a privilege to hear people speak of things which they have themselves taken part in or know from personal information. At only 9 miles from Quebec is an Indian village called Lorette inhabited by the remnants of the once powerful Hurons. But smallpox and ardent spirits, both which blessings they owe to the English together with their former bloody feuds have diminished their numbers and threatened absolute extermination. In some parts of Canada a white man who marries a squaw receives a dower with her of 50 acres of land (is that not a temptation?) So much has this intermixture of races gone on, that even at Lorette I am assured there are very few of the genuine stock, indeed one man told me only one.

The moose are of great size measuring from 7 to 8 feet to top of the shoulders. They will reach the bark from the trees 12 feet high. Many are killed for the sake of the skins, that of the legs forms good boot tops or overalls. The flesh is apt to give dysentery. Trout is found in immense quantities in the lakes North of Quebec. The best time is October, the best bait grass-hoppers, or the spawn of the fish themselves.

The banks of the St Lawrence from Quebec to Montreal are low and tame. Small villages are seen the whole distance. My next destination is Ogdensburg to which there is no conveyance till 6 tomorrow morning. Travelling at this time of the year is uncertain in the North. The navigation of the rivers closes on 1st December. The boats on the lakes I am told run till about the end of next month. I hope they will go till I have done or I shall be in a fix.The rate is higher in winter. The summer fare from M to Q is only $2. I paid $4 which includes meals and the trip only takes about 10 hours. You may guess how mild the weather is when I tell you that cattle are still out in the fields. The people of both places are very busy getting their goods off, every day is precious and craft of all kinds are employed for freight. One night of frost might put a stop to their operations.

This letter will not reach you at the usual interval but I find it impossible when on the road to write regularly. It is only when I come to a full stop like this that I have the leisure. You must also excuse any incoherence or repetition as I may not always remember what I have written. I shall be in the States on Thanksgiving Day. From Ogdensburg I intend going to Syracuse and Oswego, both in New York State, and then crossing the Lake to Kingston, then to the West. The Baltimore at which Geo. Homes resides must be in Maryland and not Canada West as Mary Ann wrote to me. If Mrs Homes does not direct her letters better they can never reach their destination. I am vexed at not receiving any letters. I directed them to be sent to Troy, Montreal and Toronto. None had arrived when I left Troy. I left orders for them to be sent here but none have come to hand. I shall leave the crossing of this page at present as I shall not send till Saturday.

St Lawrence Hotel, Ogdensburg 9.0 p.m.

I met Mr Moss again at dinner on Tuesday. This morning I was up at ½ p 4 and off by rail at 6 to Rouse's Point, 47 miles. There the train for Ogdensburg started while the Customs House Officer was examining my luggage, and I had the felicity of waiting 4½ hours in the wilderness. I believe these tricks are done on purpose to serve an hotel there. It gave me a chance of getting a good dinner. At ½ p 12 I proceeded forward to my destination, 118 miles and arrived about 6. A gentleman who left Montreal at ½ p 10 came in the same train. There are new clearings at intervals all the way. Only one place of any importance called Malone and it promises to be considerable as there is good water power and excellent land. One great novelty I saw, viz. a pump worked the same as a windmill. The gates are also hung in a singular manner by a lever. The top bar is a long pole fitted on a pivot in the gatepost, the heavy end projecting some way and weighted at the end with stones.

The country is rather flat for about 40 miles from Rouse Point. The rest is undulating and when cultivated will be very pleasant and productive. I have already done here as there are only two importers of our goods in the place and am ready to start by the boat in the morning, which is most fortunate as tomorrow she makes her last trip for the season. The alternative would be a rough ride by stage to Watertown, 60 miles before I could get the rail for Oswego. It is rather colder tonight, a little sleet has fallen and made the plank causeways as slippery as glass. Thanksgiving Day tomorrow which I shall spend on river St Lawrence and Lake Ontario. Goodnight, I have yet to write Mr Brown – as I must leave my letters for the Saturday steamers in the post office here.

I remain dearest Father and Mother, yours most affectionately

Jno. S. Webb

No. 15 Charlotte, New York State Dec1/53

Dear Mary Ann,

Your letter of 14th September came to hand on 2nd November and contains useful and opportune information. I have at last learned where Baltimore CW is, and as my next destination is Cobourg I shall most likely see Mr Holmes and perhaps spend Sunday with him. The distance of Baltimore from Cobourg is only 4 miles.

I found the cold very severe at Ogdensburg, indeed the only winter I have yet met with. On Thursday 24th I went down to the steamboat "Bay State" at 9 A.M. and was there kept prisoner till 5 P.M. not daring to leave the boat for fear of being left myself. At 5 the steamboat "British Queen" from Montreal for which they were waiting, not being arrived, it was determined not to go till 11 p.m. I therefore went back to the hotel till after supper slept on board and finally started at ½ p12 midnight, but it being the last trip of the season the delays at the stopping places were long, and at Kingston we were laid till $\frac{1}{2}$p 8 on Saturday morning and arrived at Oswego, 175 miles, at $\frac{1}{2}$ p 3 in the afternoon. For this precious long trip I paid only $5 and had my bed and board all the time. The tediousness of these delays were in some measure releaved by the sociability of the passengers. I spent the Sunday in Oswego at the Oswego Hotel. I attended the Episcopal Church near the hotel morning and night and another across the river in the afternoon. The day was very fine. This city suffered severely in the summer from a large fire but the damages are almost repaired and fine brick blocks have taken the place of wood. I left for Syracuse, 35 miles, on Monday morning at 8 a.m., dined at Globe Hotel, called on the trades and was off again for Rochester at $\frac{1}{2}$ p 1, put up at the Congress Hotel. On Tuesday 29th I went at night to the Corinthian Hall to hear a lecture by the Honble. Joshua Hargreaves on the wrongs of the exiles of Georgia. It was in favour of abolition and was received with applause. On Wednesday morning I found Jno Moulson at the breakfast table. I left for Charlotte, 7 miles, at 20 p 9 a.m. that being the mouth of the river from which place the boat starts across the lake. I was fated to another long delay and here I am yet at 12 Thursday noon as far from Cobourg as ever. This is only a small village with nothing to take away the tediousness but one or two in the same fix. Rochester is a fine city of 50,000 with very fine churches and public buildings. You must not judge of American cities by the number of the inhabitants, the people possess a great amount of public spirit of which there is ocular demonstration wherever I go. This is especially the case with churches of which there are two even in Charlotte where there are only a very few houses.

Cobourg C.W. Dec. 2nd 1853

The boat did not get to Charlotte till 9 o'clock last night. We left in it at 10 this morning. You may guess my impatience but as it could not be helped I made the best of it. There were many others waiting besides me and I passed the time in making the acquaintance with them all, especially a young lady and gentleman and two of his friends, all from Brooklyn. Also three Darkies going to settle in Canada. A little girl also in the hotel who was glad of a bit of play. Anything indeed to pass the time, but after all they were two (too) long days. The passage I found no pleasanter. The water was rather rough and made me sea sick. The distance is only 70 miles and it was accomplished in 6½ hours. We got in at ½ p 4 P.M. and I proceeded to the Globe Hotel where I partook of a comfortable supper and have had a nice chat with an Irish gentlemen who is now walking about as if he wanted a little more. This is not a large place but is progressing and promises well. If the boat goes to Toronto tomorrow night I shall have time to do my business and seek out G. Holmes. I have heard nothing of him yet and am afraid he is not there.

Russell's Hotel, Toronto C.W. Dec. 7/53

I found cousin George on Saturday. After I had finished in Cobourg I drove over to Baltimore in a buggy, dined with him and brought him to Cobourg where he spent Sunday with me. He has given up farming and now keeps a country store of groceries, crockery, dry goods, clocks, nails, tin ware, &c &c &c. He and a relative, Mr Ullin (whose sister married Mr Scrope Fowler) are in partnership and have carried on trade since June. He has a new store building which will be ready in two months. His business is but small though he realises large profits. He is still single and complains much of wanting society. I do not wonder at that; if I lived out of the world as he does I should soon be ready for a mad house. It has had a manifest effect upon him as his manners and appearance are quite rusticated. He has written you himself on this sheet. The neighbourhood of Baltimore is like some parts of Derbyshire, hilly and rugged but not in the backwoods as he said. We went together on Sunday morning to the English Church. This edifice deserves some notice. An elegant white brick church has been built over the old one in which the service is still held. All is finished but the interior so that when the old church is taken out the new one will be ready in a very short time. At night we went to the Methodist Church. On Monday morning we drove to Port Hope, 7 miles, where I had business and at 4 p.m. George drove back to Cobourg and left me waiting for the boat. No boat came that night but on Tuesday morning at ½ p 7 just as I got to the pier it came in sight and passed on at 50 yards distance without stopping. I was not very sorry for the lake was so rough and with stiff wind blowing ashore that it had required all my resolution to make up my mind to go. I returned to the hotel for breakfast and started by the stage at ¼ p 9 a.m. The distance is 65 miles and part of the road was

74

much better than I expected. The weather was wet and dull preventing a clear view of the country which, however, presented nothing remarkable but the distinctive features of zig-zag fences, tree-stumps standing thick in the fields except in old farms or such as belonged to wealthy proprietors, pine trees, log huts, a little hamlet or village at intervals and sometimes but rarely a substantial planked farmhouse tastefully built and red painted, and enclosed by ornamental fences. Also some brick houses of the same stamp. Some of the farms in high cultivation and containing fields of wheat contrasting by its rich green with the withered and wintry aspect around. Other farms so filled with stumps and stones that it is wonderful how a plough can be used in them at all. We had not the road all to ourselves for we passed or met many of the country wagons. Don't imagine a great tilted affair with six horses but a long open shallow box on four wheels with a seat in front on which you may see one or two Canadians with great rough coats, sometimes of buffalo skin, fur caps and gauntlets up the elbows, looking as if they had come down from Sir Jno Franklin's ships. Between 1 and 2 o'clock we got to Bowmanville where we dined and supped at Mr Noble's Inn at 8. Our number at this time was 8 inside and 1 out, beside the driver and we carried also a quantity of baggage and the mail. The weight therefore was considerable. When about 14 miles from Toronto as we were going up hill the leaders got loose and off they ran. Out we all jumped and had to wait in the mud till the driver caught them. He was not long and we were soon on the way but when 5 miles from our destination one of the springs broke and we all had to lend a hand to repair the coach. We got some pieces of wood for levers and then pushed in another piece between the coach and the axle on the lame side as a bearer. In this style we had to go the rest of the way and arrived safely at ¼ p 12 midnight after a most tedious journey of 15 hours with scarcely room to sit. I put up at Russell's Hotel which belongs to the same man who keeps the Hotel in Quebec. On my arrival I got letters from Father and Mother, George, Elizabeth and Sam besides Mr Brown's, which I gladly read half asleep as I was.

I dined with my friend Mondelet yesterday at his snug residence and was introduced to his wife. She is a quiet but amiable lady, unfortunately rather deaf but they appear to be very happy. We had dinner at 6; goose and roast beef; tea at 9 at which I partook of a novelty; preserved pumpkin. The evening passed in music and conversation. Mondelet plays the violin and *Letitia* the piano. I have seen Wilson, my voyage-mate, and Mr Champion who has invited me to dine with him today. The weather is still mild for the season, a little frosty, which scarcely lasts the day. The natives say there is a marked difference in the climate in late years, not being near so cold as formerly. I have business engagements for morning and tomorrow noon propose going to Hamilton. I do not think I shall get further before Monday. What do you think of George Holmes going 150 miles for dinner? It beats our Brooklynites hollow, who however think little of 20 miles to an evening party. Cousin George told me to be sure to remember him to you but his own letter will be sufficient for that.

    With best love, I remain, yours most truly, Jno S. Webb

Baltimore Cobourg Dec 4/1853

My dear Mary Ann,

    Wonders never cease, your Bro John has found me out at last in the backwoods of Canada. I have often thought of you and your kindness when a child and never expected to see you or your family again but if I am spared to see 1855 I shall make a point of coming to see you. I am doing very well in my present business after trying various employments. I am going to a Christmas dinner about 150 miles from here and then shall spend New Year in Toronto.

    I shall hope to hear from you as soon as an opportunity will afford; Kind regards to Bro George, also give my kind love to my Father and Mother when you write.

    Accept the same yourself.
From Yr Affectionate Cousin
George M. Holmes.

No. 18   18 Clinton St. Brooklyn,   Dec. 30/53

Dear Parents,

    I have no less than four letters, or rather five from you yet unanswered. You misunderstood my meaning when I said I hoped to bring company home. My home is now America and when I visit England, if my prospects admit of it, should wish to have some members of my family to share it with me. In answer to Father's of Nov. 3rd, Mr Cook keeps a store up town, similar to Cox's Church St., but on a larger scale, and is an Englishman, a cockney, I believe. He has been out 20 years or more and is going well. Crookes is a Sheffielder, son of the late – Marshall in the firm of Parkin and Marshall. He is a partner in a firm doing an extensive trade in shirts and collars which they manufacture by means of sewing machines. Their factory is in Newark, New Jersey and their store in New York, He was formerly master of the Lancasterian School in Sheffield. There was a Gamble came by one of the steamers but not the one I expected from Sheffield. I do not like Mr Sandford's style of letter writing. I have not yet answered him, but will shortly. Now for Mother's of Nov. 10th received in Pittsburgh Dec. 17th. The larger portrait was taken on 12th October, the other on 24th, both at Rees & Co's Broadway, New York.

I have not got the letter from the school which you mentioned. If it is directed to Brooklyn without reference to Long Island or New York its delivery is uncertain as there are many Brooklyns in the States. By the bye, father has not answered my query about the iron wire mentioned in mine of 27th October. Please to get me some information about it. You dear mother are equally anxious to know about the Cooks. They have shown me great kindness which I hope I know better than to abuse. The young lady has, I believe, some partiality for me but only after the New York style id. est. she would marry me if she could get no better partner. I have many friends but none I can open my heart to without reserve. Dear mother, I never knew how to prize you until now. Oh how happy I should be to have you here. "Beatrice" is a novel and consequently not fact per ipse but I doubt not truth has ever exceeded its details.

Dr Kennedy's church is Episcopalian Methodist which corresponds with the Wesleyan body in England, but with a different form of government. Mr Belcher had two little pigs which fared no better than your partridge. I wish you would not feel anxious about me, you make yourselves miserable about nothing. I guess you have all your big children at home now, except Benjamin. I was quite worried that I could not send any letters so as to reach you at Xmas or New Year. Please to take the will for the deed as I could "not fix it nohow". You would think me "real mean". Anyhow I was "pretty extensive" to George and Sue. I am afraid you must be "dreadful tired" of reading my letters. Thanks for your best love, when did I get ought else; also your good wishes which I most heartily exchange with you. May this New Year be fraught with every blessing to you which can make life happy.

I find I am quite in arrears with my journal as I have given no account of myself since 7th Dec. The next day was Sunday. The rain during the night had changed into snow and the streets of Pittsburgh were in a very slippery condition. In the morning I went to St Peter's Episcopal Church, a very handsome new stone building. Monday 19th was stormy, snowing all the day. At night the sleighs began to make their appearance and next day were in general use. Wednesday at 9 a.m. I left Pittsburgh for Harrisburg the seat of government for the state of Pennsylvania, distance 251 miles. The country through which the rail passed is of a most wild and interesting character. It passes across the Allegheny Mountains which rise steep and precipitous, the narrow valleys between are like ravines. The Americans do not care to bore tunnels where they can use other means. Hence the many and sharp curves to avoid hills. But on this route they have recourse to another expedient, a series of inclined planes up and down which the cars are separately carried by pulleys worked by a stationary engine at the extremity. I confess I felt some doubt of their safety at the first ascent but that *marvelled* (vanished) on reaching the top. The rope is made of wire which like the bundle of sticks is strong by its intimate union. The latter part of the last descent is so gentle that the cars go by themselves. These breaks in the onward progress caused some delay and at Holidaysburg we had to stay an hour and a half for a train coming in so that when we arrived at our destination it was 20 past 1 next morning. I put up at the United States Hotel and not having many calls to make I went forward by the 2 p.m. train to Baltimore, 82 miles, and through direct to Washington, 40m. The seat of the national government is in Washington and of course the Capitol is the great object of interest with strangers. It is a splendid building of white marble. In the rotundo are large pictures of National interest and a fine room with two galleries filled with books. I took my seat in both houses; that is the senate which answers to our Lords and the House of Representatives which is the American Commons. The grounds are neatly laid out with broad gravel walks and well kept. There is some fine statuary at the entrances to the buildings. From the Capitol the avenues broad and planted with trees

78

diverge in every direction. At the end of one of them is the President's house which I have not had time to see. The new monument to Washington is in rapid progress and already lifts its head a considerable height. I visited also the Patent Office, a noble building similar in style to the British Museum. It contains besides models of everything patented by the American government, numerous curiosities and relics. Here is the dress worn by Washington, war-like instruments, domestic utensils, masks and toys from China, the Fejees Islands, etc., a large collection of specimens in natural history, geology, concology etc. After viewing these I returned to my hotel (Gadsby's) and left 23rd 5 p.m. for Baltimore. On the way I fell into conversation with a blind gentleman from St Louis and was astonished by the extent of his information and his vivid description of various parts of The States. I found however that his blindness must have been of recent date though I forbore asking him on the subject. We put up at the same hotel in Baltimore, the Entaw House, I was much amused by his conduct at supper. Like all Southerners and slave holders he expected implicit obedience from the waiters and having ordered one to fix and season his eggs, the man who, I guess, did not observe his want of sight, pertly said that he could not fix them to his liking. My companion instantly jumped to his feet and taking up his chair, threatened to knock him down, saying if he had a pistol he would shoot him. He told me afterwards that he had once shot at one of his slaves but the pistol fortunately missed fire. Finding he could not restrain himself, he prudently gave up keeping any slaves.

Baltimore presented a most lively appearance on Saturday 24th. Evergreens and garlands for decorating and all the stores made to look as tempting as possible to invite the attention of the numerous buyers. At one hardware store at which I called I found a grave gentleman employed in making a Christmas tree while his partner was busy finishing a toy chair to hang upon it. I spent a most delightful Sunday[*] with Miss Perrigow and her family. Accompanied her and her sister Maria to Entaw St. Methodist Church in the morning, to Grace Episcopal Church in the afternoon and Westminster Presbyterian Church at night. I left their house at $\frac{1}{4}$ p 10 with the feeling that it had been one of my happiest days in America. I

[*] it seems odd that he does not call Sunday December 25th Christmas Day.

took the ½ p 8 o'clock train next morning for New York, arrived in Philadelphia 99 miles at ½ p 12, staid to dine and forward to Amboy, 63 miles, at 2 o'clock; then by boat "John Potter", 27 miles to New York, arrived ½ p 6. My friends seemed glad to have me back, they had almost given me up as lost. Having got home you must let me rest awhile. So goodbye for the present and think of me as your affectionate son Jno S. Webb

No. 16   18 Clinton St. Brooklyn   Jan 10th, 1854

Dear Mary Ann,

Though the date of my letter to our parents was Jan 3[rd.] yet I only give my account up to the 26th. The new year commences with the greatest holiday observed in America, or at least in New York. The 4th July is very much thought of but of course the English cannot participate much in that birthday of independence.

I called at my friends the Cook's on Thursday 29th who appeared very glad to see me back. Friday 30th I went to Paterson. On Saturday to Newark and spent New Year's Eve there with Mr Crookes and Misses Marshall, returned by the 11 train and was so nigh run for time that I had to jump in while it was going. The alternative would have been to stay all night which I did not wish at all as I longed to spend Sunday at home. On Sunday morning I went to Washington St. Church with Milner. Dr Kennedy preached. I staid at home in the afternoon and at night went with Milner to St. John's Epl. Ch. Rev. Mr Guion preached but his sermon contrasted very unfavourably with the doctor's, though on the same subject, a retrospect of the year. It consisted chiefly of politics and he sent us all over the world, but not a bit of the way to heaven. Sawyer, Littlewood and Milner spent the night with me.

On Monday morning everybody prepared to spend the day according to custom. The ladies had no doubt been doing so some time and now nothing remained to do but to set things in order and make themselves as charming as possible ready for their levées. The gentlemen with their best Sunday clothes and long lists of lady friends set off gaily on their pleasure tour. Business was for the time lost sight of & dollars & cents only remembered to be spent in reckless profusion. Snow having fallen the

Thursday before, sleighs had been used for several days and were of course, on this occasion in great request. One gentleman having a very handsome one with a span of fine horses was offered $100 or more than £20 for the loan of it during the day. At the livery stables $50 were asked in many instances, the streets were resonant with sleigh bells. It was a stirring time I can tell you.

Well, you will want to know what I did. Same as the rest, of course. I started off to New York about 10 AM. Called on the Dickinson's (D. is agent for Hargreaves & Co) and Cooks and was pressed to finish off at night with them which I gladly agreed to, Then returned to Brooklyn, called on Miss Cottier, Mrs Butler & Mrs Thirlbut, Miss Read, Mrs Cowlishaw. There I met Mr & Mrs Ellison & Miss Black. Miss & Mrs Patten, Mrs Dean, Mrs Clark, Misses Kennaday, Misses Thompson, the last is my boarding house but instead of entering with a latch key as usual, I rang the bell as a visitor & handed my card in. I then went back to New York & called on Mr & Mrs Marshall of the firm of Tillotson & Marshall, then went up to Cooks, got there about 10 PM and (Oh, tell it not in Gath) got home at 20 p 3 next morning. There are no meals on this day after breakfast, but wherever you go you find the table groaning under all sorts of viands with coffee, lemonade, wine & spirits, and it is expected that you will partake of them.

On Wednesday night I went up with Milner to the Crystal Palace. This is the last time it is to be opened after 5.0 pm. Thursday night I attended Class with Sawyer & Littlewood & spent the night with Milner in Mr Hoodless's room. He is one of my fellow boarders. Both Friday and Saturday nights I spent in my own room with Sawyer. Sunday morning and night I went to Dr Kennaday's Church. In the afternoon I waited according to appointment for Littlewood calling to accompany him to School, but owning to some misunderstanding he did not come. At night I mustered quite a large party in my little room. Harmer, Sawyer, Littlewood & Milner. These are very pleasant reunions which I enjoy very much. The latter is with me almost continually. He has left Cottiers and has now a room at our house. Littlewood is going a journey West which will take him about six weeks & then I expect he will take Sawyer's room, who is leaving next Monday to go to Cowlishaw's. By the bye, one of us is engaged to an amiable & pious American lady. So much for an oft expressed resolve not to marry any but English. Do not be alarmed it is not me. Harmer has quite recovered the effects of the fall from his horse. He left off the plasters yesterday.

Josh Milner is with Tillotsons & will probably go to California for them by & bye. The two Germans have left our house & in consequence the supper table has undergone a thaw. The terrible winter predicted by my friends has yet to come as yet I have felt no inconvenience.

There was a fire in New York early on Sunday morning which did considerable damage. The Lafarge Hotel & Metropolitan Hall, a splendid mass of marble buildings were laid in ruins. The former was to be opened for the first time on Thursday next, the latter has been used as a concert & lecture Hall. Gavarre was the last to use it. He lectured there on Thursday & Friday nights and on Saturday embarked for England. The loss will be nearly a million of dollars. New York has suffered very much the last two months by fire. One of them set fire to three ships lying in the docks one of which "The Great Republic" was the largest clipper ship ever built just ready for the first voyage. Her tonnage was about 4500 tons.

I must not forget to tell you that I received your two letters. You get your money monthly now, do you not? I mentioned it to Mr Brown some time ago. The last letter Elizth. sent me is the best she has written. I was delighted with it. I am sorry you do not like your scamp of a brother. I will tell you how the portrait happened to be taken in so ungraceful an attitude. Milner & I went together & while we were waiting our turn amused ourselves by putting our hair into all sorts of shapes & when called for found no comb to straighten it again, so in I went with my hat on & determined to have a portrait which, as the man said, was full of character; too full, it appears, for you!

Last night I had quite a time. Sawyer & Littlewood went to a party at Mr Musgrave's in Fulton St. Brooklyn, and Mr Clark through whom they had become acquainted, was specially requested to invite me. I went and found more than forty. We had a pleasant evening and did not break up till $\frac{1}{2}$ p 2. I of course gallantly offered to escort one of the young ladies and unfortunately considering the late hour, pitched upon one who lived the farthest off. It was 25 to 4 before I got home.

With much love, I remain your affy

Jno S. Webb

15 Gold St. New York   Jany 11th 1854

Dear Elizth.

Since I wrote to you last I have received your two letters. I am sorry I have not got them here that I might read them over before I write this. I have the greatest pleasure in giving you such praise as the last deserves. It is beautifully written & evidently denotes that much pains have been taken. The other is not so good. I am glad to see you striving to improve & hope you will not be weary in it.

I have not time to say much this morning & my mind is also occupied with other matters. I was afraid you would be disappointed if I delayed any longer. How have you passed the holidays? The young people here have much shorter ones, not more than a fortnight. They have more in the hot weather. Santa Claus has filled many stockings with various gifts. One young lady was quite vexed to find a little cabbage in hers and called him hard names for his meanness.

The East river was full of ice last night, in large fragments they come down the north river or Hudson & are brought in by the tide. Two men in a little boat were pulling themselves along by the ice, not being able to row in the usual manner. You must not think it is very cold. I go along the streets with my coat unbuttoned. I have had two or three tumbles, the ice on the sidewalks has been very slippery. There was a thaw middle of week which filled the roads full of duck ponds.

I remain dearest, Your loving uncle Jno S. Webb

No. 19 P

18 Clinton St. Brooklyn   Feby 3rd 1854

Dear Parents,

Since writing last I have received yours of 29th & 30th Dec. on Jan 16th and of Jan 5 on the 26th. I spent Christmas Day quite happily as you already know in a pleasant family circle where I felt quite at home. Its being the Sabbath did not prevent its innocent enjoyment, for religion hallows & purifies instead of impairing our pleasures.

A severe winter is generally a prelude to a good harvest. You have the one and I hope will realise the other. The weather here has been changeable. Yesterday was like summer, today we have snow and frost. There has been so much ice in the East river at times that several ferry boats have been disabled by it. But this mischief is nothing compared with that occasioned by the devouring element of fire in the city. Scarcely a night has passed over for some time past which has not been signalised by the alarm bells and firemen running hither and thither, the loss of property and in some cases of life. The most dreadful instance of the latter took place at Ravenswood near Astoria, Long Island. Seventeen persons were blown up in a cartridge factory and the bodies so mangled that some could not be recognised.

On Sunday night a fire occurred in Duane St New York by which 100 families were turned almost naked into the street. There were two other fires the same night. These are only examples. To tell you all would be tedious both to you & me.

On Tuesday 24th Milner met me after business in the Clinton Library and we took tea at Thompson's saloon Broadway then proceeded up to Cooks. They had asked me to tea but I do not like to sponge, you know. Miss C. and I then went to the Tabernacle to hear Lucy Stone on anti-slavery. I was much pleased with the lecture which was listened to by a large and attentive audience. Miss Stone is rather plain both in face & dress. She wore a cloth habit and pants with a very small collar & her hair puff.

On Friday having business up town I got into one of the Eighth avenue cars & on arriving at my destination I was so anxious to get out that I did not wait till it had stopped. The consequence was that, losing my balance, but not my hold of the car, I was so dragged through the mud as to spoil my overcoat & had to be measured for a new one which has cost me $16. I went into an oyster saloon close by & was washing & brushing all morning.

On Sunday morning Littlewood, Milner & I went to the Pilgrims church, in the afternoon I went over to NY with Milner to Quakers Meeting and at night I went to Washington St. church and staid to prayer meeting.

On Monday I went on a goosechase in search of customers as far as Dover NJ 44 miles, staid there all night & returned on Tuesday much disappointed. Saw a man cutting ice by hand with a cross cut saw. Scraped acquaintance with a young lady in the car which made the journey back more agreeable.

The Parliament House in Quebec was burnt down last Wednesday.

With best wishes, I remain Yr. Affect son

Jno S. Webb

No. 17 MA   18 Clinton St. Brooklyn   Feby 3rd 1854

Dear Mary Ann,

I am attempting to do what you will not thank me for: to write when I have nothing to say

. . . .

When gentlemen call on ladies they are not entertained by a host of father, mother, brothers, sisters &c but they are received by the lady alone & the tête a tête is uninterrupted by any other party. Only think you see me ringing at the door of a smart looking house where I have never been before, but to take home one of the lady tenants. A servant comes to the door to whom I hand my card & am ussured [sic] into the parlour. After a while in comes the lady with smiling face ready to listen to anything. What a dangerous situation, is it not? First topic the weather, 2nd the health, 3rd the news, 4th coming events, 5th mutual friends, 6th poetry & music which is perhaps diversified by the piano forte & a song, 7th you feel ready to enter on most delicate & tender subjects, or if a prudent man make your exit, when the lady expresses her sorrow that you are obliged to go, and asks you to come again soon and keeps you a little longer to shew you those beautiful flowers or that exquisite little basket. Then with a gentle pressure of the hand and a tender look in the eye you take your departure. Some families are exceptions to this practice as the Cooks, Kennadys &c, though in all cases private conversation is practicable as the parlours consist of two rooms opening into each other by folding doors. Give me however the old country style & the dear girls of my native land.

I see I have accomplished my wish of filling this side anyhow, & it remains only to express to you my good wishes for your happiness and assure you of the lasting love & affection of your own brother.

Kisses all round for the children.

John S. Webb

No. 20 P   15 Gold St New York   March 7th '54

My dear Parents,

I received Mother's 3 Kind letters.

. . . .

I have sent my circulars out for a journey which will take me a considerable time, so it strikes me that time present will be the best to write to you, lest I should not find so good an opportunity in the future. I fully intended sleeping last night in one of the magnificent Sound steamers on my way to Boston but a consignment of goods arrived last week & I am obliged to remain a little longer to put them through the Customs.

My stay in Boston will be four or five days & on my return, I shall proceed on a tour of which the proposed route is as follows: Albany, Troy, Schenectady, Syracuse, Rochester, Buffalo, Cleveland, Pittsburgh, Wheeling, Columbus, Cincinatti, Frankfort, Louisville, Madison, Indianopolis, Dayton, Toledo, Detroit, London, Hamilton, Toronto, Port Hope, Coburg Kingston, Ogdensburg, Montreal, Quebec & home through the state of Maine. In this list are twelve cities I have not yet visited. I may see fit to extend or contract but I do not think it will take me less than three months. I have almost determined to give up my room which will save me two dollars a week.

So much for the future DV. Now for the past. I know you like to know every particular & I try my best to gratify you. On the 24th I went up to the Menagerie in Broadway to see the wild animals. The Siamese twins and a little boy who bids fair to exceed Tom Thumb in littleness being four years old & weighs only six pounds. The collection is small & consists of an elephant, rhinoceros, Alpaca, a few tigers, lions, leopards, a hyena, a wild cat, monkeys, parrots, cockatoos. A man enters a cage where is a lion, lioness & three leopards & goes through a number of manoeuvres. I had some conversation with the twins. If I remember right they are 42 years old, are both married, two sisters having been smitten with their charms, which by the bye are not very great. One has six & the other five children, two of which I saw.

Sat. 25th. I spent the evening at home with Milner. Sunday was a very wet day. The rain pouring down in torrents. In the afternoon M & I ventured out to Trinity Church where we found about a score men and one lady.

1874 The Siamese Twins

JANUARY 22, 1874

An American telegram announces the death of two brothers whose career offers a pregnant illustration of the distinction drawn by Dr. Johnson between notoriety and fame. The publicity attained by the persons in question was literally worldwide; and it is very probable that their collective, if not their individual, appellation has been familiar for two generations among races who had never heard of the most renowned statesmen, philosophers, poets or painters of Europe or the United States.

The extraordinary peculiarity which marked their physical conformation rendered them alike an object of curiosity to crowned heads and to the most ignorant of sightseers. Had they been born apart, few people would have cared a rush about them, but with that singular bond of union between them they could not fail to rivet the attention of the public. At length they have been liberated from perhaps the most dolorous and most painfully borne captivity that ever fell to the lot of much-suffering human kind.

It was telegraphed yesterday from Philadelphia that Chang and Eng died on Saturday last at the age of 63 years at their home in North Carolina. They had long since enjoyed all the advantages of American citizenship, and assumed the characteristic surname of Bunker.

They were, according to report, decent, unobtrusive men; and, strange to relate, they were married and each of them had numerous children. As Chang and Eng, two quiet Chinamen,—for it is extremely dubious whether they came from Siam— who spent the autumn of their lives as tobacco planters in a remote part of the United States, they may speedily fade away from public recollection; but they will have a permanent abiding place side-by-side with the Irish Giant and the Polish Dwarf, the Aztec children, and the more or less apocryphal Pig-faced Lady in the "Wonderful Museum" as the Siamese Twins.

15

On Saturday night after reading a while M & I went down to see Littlewood who cut both of our portraits from shadows on the wall for himself. On my returning home I fixed up one he had previously cut of me on the wall putting black paper behind it & it is I assure you a first rate portrait.

I was introduced to Mr Knickerbocker on Sunday, a descendant of one of the oldest Dutch settlers. His father is wealthy & lives at Scaghticoke on the Hudson where he can shew buildings on his farm upwards of 200 years old. He is also proud of shewing his furniture which though antique is singularly like the present mode. Fashion you know runs its circle and justifies Solomon's words that there is nothing new under the sun. He had, much to his regret, lost his family Bible, but one day he happened to call upon some old people & there he saw one which seemed to be a *thundering* old one. He asked the old man if he would sell it, and he was referred to the dame. She said yes, she guessed he might have it, so he took out a five dollar bill & asked her if that would do. She assented, so anxious lest she should change her mind; he got hold of it and carried it home *straight ahead,* not suffering anyone to touch it. When there he examined his treasure & found in it a register of all the births, marriages & deaths that had occurred in S for 200 years, his own family included. It was bound in boards id est real wooden boards, and the back being in want of repair, it was sent to the *blacksmith* for that purpose, which was effected *with an iron hoop.*

Mr K. Junr. has been brought up to the law but not liking the profession, he intends commencing in Broadway, New York as a publisher.

Mrs Cook told me a very affecting incident connecting the family of the Miss Cassidy's, the ladies I took home from the sewing meeting at her home. They had a brother, steady & pious, esteemed by all who knew him. He had for some time been in a low state of health & spirits and not able to sleep well at night, on which account his chamber was chosen next to his mother's so that she could hear him if he wished for anything in the night. About two years ago they had some company and did not retire till 12 o'clock about two hours after him. Before his mother went into her own room, she called in to see if he was asleep and was rejoiced to find he was. In the morning it was discovered that he had left half-draped, but thinking he might have put other clothes on, and taken a walk before

88

breakfast it was not thought much of, but meal after meal passed with no tidings and after sitting up the whole night they put advertisements in the papers and notified all his friends. All to no effect, he has never been heard of to this day. It is supposed that in a fit of melancholy he walked down to the dock and into the water, and his body carried away by the tide.

On Monday 6th I met Mr Crookes and he pressed me to go to Newark, so I started off in the afternoon, and after seeing my customers there, I took tea with him and his sisters, took a walk with the latter after tea and stayed all night. He is very wishful for me to come and live with him, and if I was always at home it would be as cheap, for I could commute with the R.Rd. Co. for $50 per an, and my board would be that less. I returned to New York this morning.

My prospect for the coming year is a moving one, I expect to be travelling most of the time. I have made up my mind about my room, and as Littlewood called to go to dine with me, I offered it to him from Tuesday next. I see no good in paying $2 a week all the time I am away, though I grieve to leave so snug a spot. Within a week from this day last year, I started with hope and expectation in my heart for the unknown country, & though I have not yet realised my hopes and succeeded in my expectations I still hope, and not without reason. I should not like to live in Sheffield again, though to visit it I should feel is a thing I dearly hope to do.

An immense quantity of flour has been shipped for England. You might have been starved out if Brother Jonathan had not assisted you. You have, dear mother, a right to ask any questions you like. I of course shall reserve the option of answering them. Young Moss was acquitted in the case of stabbing, being justified on the plea of self defence, but in the course of investigations, facts came out which stamped his character unfavourably. Though he possesses a diploma of M.D. he has found it necessary to seek a situation and amongst others he applied to me.

Gavarre has I see been electrifying our townsmen with his opinions on American slavery. He is right to a certain extent. The immediate abolition of slavery would be no benefit to them in their present state of ignorance. The best way for the legislature to do would be to declare all children born of slaves, from this time to be free, and after a period of so many years to free the adults also. Preparations should in the mean time be made for this event, a system of slave education extended through the slave states suited to their capacities and asylums built for the young. But I fear such an event is not fixed for an early day. The further extension of the accursed system is contemplated and striven for by bipeds who would fain be called men.

The Library out of which I have had my books is to be removed to Eighth Street, which will be most inconvenient for me by reason of the distance. But I may live up there when I come back from my travels. Scott and Moulson live there but they pay more than I can afford $8½ per week each. I must now come to a conclusion.

From your affec. and dutiful son,

Jno S. Webb

No. 21   18 Clinton St. Brooklyn   Mch 30/54

My dear Parents,

You will be surprised to find my letter dated from here, but I have been fully occupied this week and impatient as I am to be off, I am constrained to stay till the commencement of another week. I have been busy receiving goods and packing off orders, for as I am to be absent so long I have many arrangements to make so as to leave all straight. It is very inconvenient for me that the removal time takes place when it will be impossible for me to be in New York, but time and tide for no man bide, and I must make the best of existing circumstances. The weather has been very cold this week and this afternoon snow began to fall. The season is however fast advancing and I expect before long to be complaining of the heat.

Your paltry collections contrast strongly with the liberal open-handed way in which church expenses are met here. Last Sunday after service the treasurer gave a statement of the liabilities which the trustees had to meet amounting to $678. A collection was then made and parties not being prepared with the amount they wish to give, stated the sum. The whole amount was realised. Three individuals gave $100 each.

Do not be anxious about me I am very cautious and prudent taking great care of myself as I have none to divert my attention from number one. I am glad to hear that the iron wire is not forgotten.

I am going D.V. by the 5 PM train to Albany. John Moulson is anxious about his brother who is in the "City of Glasgow" steamer now in her 34th day out. I have received two papers, the Sheffield Examiner and the Weekly Times for which I am obliged. I am looking for letters by the Baltic now due.

Much love to all from your own John.

No. 22   United States Hotel, Milwawkee, Wis   May 3/54

My very dear Parents,

Here is a strange contradiction: viz: the further I go from home the nearer it is to me. Our spirits or souls rather, arc not separated by distance.

In answer to your questions: The sewing meetings are now over for the season. The gentlemen do not attend till towards nine o'clock which gives time for work, though you are right in thinking there is little done after their arrival. Milner is indeed a good hearted fellow and ready to do anything for me, a real friend, very fond of reciting poetry of which he has treasured some choice specimens. I do not know what I should do without him when at home: we read, talk, walk and think together and it is through his kindness that I have been able to save the expense of keeping a room without depriving myself of a home. A short residence in America has marvellously improved him. He arrived from England on the 12th August last (the hottest day we had during the year) by the unfortunate steamer "City of Glasgow", now out from England 60 days without any tidings of her with 300 passengers on board among whom is one of Mr Jno Moulson's sons and brother to my friend Mr Moulson of New York. Milner is in the employment of Tillotson & Marshall and if their Californian business requires it, will have to go out to assist Mr Harmer.

I will now give you some further account of my journey from where I left off in my No. 19 to Susan.* I was in the midst of the Prairies and there I might have stopt, if it had depended on myself to get out. From the

* No. 19 is missing, as are most of his letters to Susan.

91

wooded country about Alton the rails pass through the Prairies for 160 miles and a great part of that distance not a tree or a shrub can be seen, nothing but grassland stretching all round like a lawn to the horizon. A compass, the sun, or a star, would be as much required here as at sea, it is trackless and void of land marks. There are some stations and two considerable villages, Springfield and Bloomington; the first 72, the other 131 from Alton. The land is rich and when cultivated yields a large increase. The great drawback is the want of wood. Immense tracks are still in their native state and abound in game. I saw some wild deer, cranes, curlews and turkey buzzards. We were much annoyed by cows and pigs on the rails. They mostly ran off as if their tails were on fire, when the iron monster snorted at them from a distance. Sometimes they would run along and then we would have to slack our pace. We dined at Virdenia station 50 miles from Alton and supped at Bloomington. It was between 9 & 10 when we got to La Salle, 60 miles from Bloomington and the head of the navigation on the Illinois River, down the bank of which the rails dip in an inclined plane apparently not less than 45°. The baggage van only is let down, the passengers on it if they like to ride, for my part I preferred walking. Having crossed the bridge other cars were waiting to convey us forward. La Salle is a rough looking steep place. After waiting near an hour we went forward and arrived at Chicago about three o'clock on Sunday morning. Then I proceeded in a stage to the Tremont House where they were so full of guests that I had to be content with a room in which were four beds. There I got to rest and soon forgot my fatigue. I feel rather sorry now that I did not take the route by the Mississippi River to Rock Island and thence by rails on which I should have passed the famous Morman City of Nauvoo. The front of the temple is I am told still standing and gives some idea of its former magnificence. It stands 200 miles above Alton. The river is navigable 581 miles beyond Nauvoo to a place called Fort Snelling. I was up on Sunday at 7 o'clock after three hours' sleep. Having dispatched my breakfast I sallied forth to find Mr and Mrs Horner. I found them in the upper part of a house in Randolph St, the first floor being used by some other party as a store. I had the number of the house else I should have been directed to it by a sign swinging outside which announced "Mrs Horner: Ladies' Music Store". I knocked at the door top of the steps and it being opened by Mrs H. I entered an ill furnished apartment containing a piano, table, one rocking chair, a sideboard, and two or three settees which were apparently used as beds for the children. I was asked to sit on the only chair. Mrs H expressed her pleasure at seeing a townsman, though a stranger, said her husband had not yet risen as he was suffering from a headache. His voice however soon entered the apartment from one adjoining where he was in bed, and after conversing a while I took my leave, promising to call again in the afternoon. I then proceeded to church (2nd Presbn. Wabash Ave). After dinner called on Horner. Mrs H told me she had continued her public religious meeting here till she was prevented by having her baby. She has now three children, the eldest a boy of 6½ and two girls. Lest you should be ignorant of her identity I will here state that she was a Miss Eadon, my sisters became acquainted with her at Mr Hardesty's. I believe that Mr H and I then took a walk about the city and departing at the hotel, I took tea and went in the evening to the Methodist Epis¹. Ch. in Clark St. I was ashamed of myself both at morning and evening service as I could not help nodding all the time nearly. I went early to bed. On Monday morning May 1st I called at Horner's office. He has commenced business for himself in connexion with a German. The style runs Horner & Crone, Railroad, Emigrant, Forwarding, Exchange and Real Estate Agents, 117 Clark St. Chicago, Illinois. I then went to work and in the evening wrote letters home. On Tuesday after I had got through I called again on Horner and we visited some of the principal stores, and can assure you that some of them would grace London itself. We then mounted the top of a high building and had a view of the city. It now contains 65,000 inhabitants and its trade is very considerable. It is situated in the State of Illinois, an Indian name signifying "river of men" sufficiently applicable when we consider the stream of immigration flowing into and through it. It is only about 20 years old and is rapidly increasing. By means of ship canals between the lakes it is proposed to have direct communication with the Atlantic and give it all the advantages of a seaport. The expenses of transport of goods are now heavy. After tea at the hotel I spent the evening in Mr Horner's house. I was entertained by Master Whitfield Horner playing his scales on the piano, had a good deal of gossip with Mrs Horner about the Sheffield folk, and a few songs after which I took my leave.

On Wednesday morning May 3rd I took my passage on the streamboat "E.K. Collins" for Milwaukee, 90 miles. It was a fine bright morning but cold. The water of Lake Michigan is not clear. That which

I've had to drink at the hotel looked as if milk had been mixed with it. As we got further out it assumed the most beautiful pale sea green. Gulls flew about us in great numbers and steamboats, sloops and rigs in all directions gave a charm to the vast fishpond. Talking of fish, tremendous trout are caught in this lake but they want the delicate flavour of our English river trout. The shore is bluff but even and covered with trees, still brown. I lost sweet verdant Spring on the prairies and no wonder either. We stopped at three pretty places on the Lake, Waukegon, Kenosha and Racine. At the latter place we waited near two hours. We arrived at Milwaukee at 5 and I made my temporary home at the United States Hotel. I took tea and then walked out to view the city. It is not as large as Chicago but built on higher ground and possessing excellent spring water. It is healthier.

I did not see one pretty girl in Chicago. Here there are few plain ones. I was struck with the size and beauty of a building, and entering it found myself in a R.C. Cathedral. It has been built chiefly by Austrian money. The Bishop having gone there on purpose for subscriptions. An Orphan Asylum occupies one building to the right. The papists know the advantage gained by training children. Arrived at the bluff of the hill commanding the lake I lay down on the grass and watched the flocks of wild ducks and the numerous little sail boats on the lake till the growing darkness induced me to return.

Toledo   May 6 1854

I learned by the grinding of music and large painted announcements that my fellow passengers on the Buffalo and Cleveland R.Rd. had arrived here before me. Milwaukee has 55,000 inhabitants. In 1836 the population was 700 only. It has numerous railways in process, so it may be expected to rise still more rapidly. Thursday 4th was hot but not a legitimate summer day. The air keen with the wind from the north and the sun trying to roast you all the time. On Friday 5th I left at 9 AM to return to Chicago, by steamboat "Traveller". There must have been a strong wind the night before for Lake Michigan was quite rough which fact was proved to me in an unpleasant manner. I was sick and had to lay down most of the time. A young lady allowed me to escort her to dinner on condition that I would also partake. I fulfilled my promise by swallowing a square inch of rice pudding and also accomplished about two mouthfuls of chicken. A most suitable wife for a steamboat captain, was she not? I occupied myself with the progress and practices of Mr Budgett "the Successful Merchant". But I had looked from my book many a time to admire the sweet smile, gentle carriage and mild voice of a young lady who was taking care of two children and a baby with all the tender solicitude of a mother. I now made her acquaintance and learned that she had been visiting at her brother's in Milwaukee the past eight months and was returning with his wife and little ones to Unionville between Erie and Cleveland where her mother lived. Finding them thus unprotected I took them in charge. We all went up to Sherman House on arriving in Chicago to take tea and wait for the train to Toledo. I called on a customer with whom I had an appointment, also on Mrs Horner and at 9 pm went forward by rail to Toledo 242 miles. The night was cold and the stove in the car was not lit. Some fire was put in after we started or we should have been frozen. We arrived at 8 o'clock Saturday morning and after breakfasting with the ladies and seeing their luggage right for Cleveland I bade them farewell and was almost overpowered with their thanks and pressed to visit them at Unionville. I was much disappointed with Toledo. It is a straggling place of only 9000 inhabitants. Thayer's American Hotel at which I put up and a few good buildings are at one extremity, and the business part, principal stores, landings and depot at the other as if there had been a diversity of opinion as to where the town should be. It reminds me of Shakespeare's Richard III "sent into the world not half made up". The roads are of dust and the causeways of planks. One is almost as loose as the other. The pretty river Manonee on which it is located is an ornament and abounds in splendid fish. There are also fine orchards in the vicinity now full of blossom.

With heartfelt wishes for your happiness & welfare,

Affectionately yours, Jno S. Webb

P.S.   Michigan Exchange Hotel, Detroit   May 8/54

I arrived here this afternoon and proceeded first thing to the Post Office where I got a packet of American letters but none from home & none received in N.Y. up to May 2nd. I felt much disappointed. Today is fine and bright and our trip in the steamboat "Dart" has been pleasant. The distance is 65 miles. We started at 9 AM Canada & the States almost shake hands here. Across the Detroit River is the Canadian town of Sandwich & a continuous communication is kept by a ferry boat.

Love to all from the absent member, John

No. 23   18 Clinton St. Brooklyn   8.6.54

My dear Parents,

I have been wishing to write you for several days past but as I got to the end of my journey, my anxiety to finish well kept my mind occupied and my hours employed. I had less leisure in Montreal and Quebec than in any other places. I was nursing customers local and others I met with at the hotels from the Western Province. I am glad to tell you that I have the prospect of a good trade in Canada and have made many friends there. I last wrote, to Susan, from Brockville. It was ¼ to 9 before the steamboat "Cataract" left on that night (29th), and though the distance to Ogdensburg is only 12 miles we did not arrive till ½ p 10, being delayed at two stopping places on the way. I slept at the St Lawrence Hotel, and the boat for Montreal starting early every morning, I had to stay till Wednesday. The number of customers is limited so that I had most of the day to myself. I went over the river in the steam ferryboat to Prescot. It is a mean little old-fashioned Canadian town, slow as the boat itself which took ¼ hour to go the 1½ miles. At night I took a walk in the suburbs of Ogdensburg and was much amused by a novel manner of fishing I saw practised. Here is a river running into the St Lawrence called the Oswegatelice. A short distance from its mouth it is damd. up for mill purposes causing the stream below to assume the character of a shallow rapid. It was in this part that several men and boys were engaged. Two waded into the water with a net which they spread across the stream while the others commencing higher up, ran down as fast as they could driving the fish in with long sticks. The bottom is rough with boulders and pebbles, so that often in their haste they fell flat on their faces in the water. A stick fire was burning on the bank for the purpose of warming and drying their clothes. I saw the fruits of their labours on a little pound at the edge fenced in from the stream by pebbles. There were a number of black bass, suckers, whitefish and sunfish.

At 7 AM on 31st May I took my passage on board the steamboat "British Queen" for Montreal. The morning was quite frosty but the sun soon made himself felt. This trip is the most delightful and exciting of the whole Canada route, and no-one should visit the country without taking it. The current is swift most of the way but the rapids themselves are splendid boiling and foaming and dashing with resistless force. We came to the first Le Soult at 11 AM which would make it about 50 miles on the way, next the Coteau de lac at 20 p 3 or another 50 miles then the Cedar Split rock Cascade and lastly the Lactime just before arriving in Montreal. These last are so strong and intricate that an Indian is regularly taken on board at Cangnawagu to pilot the boat through. You would be surprised to see the waves and troughs formed by the force of the water. We reached Montreal at ½ p 6 PM (distance 131 miles) and put up at Montreal House. I have stated in one of my letters that there is no rocksalt on this continent but I was informed differently by a Yorkshire engineer, Mr Gatliss, now living in Toowanda Pa. He stated that in surveying some land about six miles from Hamilton C.W. he had found it by boring about 25 feet. I met with him on the boat and happening to put up at Montreal & Quebec at the same hotel, and return to Montreal together we got quite intimate and he pressed me to go and see him in Pennsylvania. Thursday 1st June was a hot day. I was surprised and annoyed by the clouds of flies almost like moths which filled the air, covered the houses, and gave an extra coat to everybody. On enquiry found they were the shad flies preceding or coming along with the shad fish in their spring migration up the St Lawrence River. These flies are fortunately of an ephemeral nature. On my return from Quebec there were very few to be seen. I ran round to see my customers and in the evening set off to Quebec in steamboat "Lady Elgin". She has no reason to feel flattered for a dirtier, shabbier affair I have never yet ridden in. She carried us safely and being asleep most of the time I felt little inconvenience. We arrived in Quebec (180 miles) on Friday morning and I took up my temporary abode in Russell Hotel. In the evening I went up to the public promenade called the Governor's Garden, and had much pleasure in listening to two military bands who were playing there. One was a large and effective brass band, the other six Highlanders on bagpipes. I liked the former best as I have not lived long enough to appreciate the latter. I afterwards took a walk with one of my customers. The city looks quite gay with numerous triumphal arches of evergreens, raised to welcome the Governor, Lord Elgin. He is a great favourite with the French Canadians, as he treats them with great favour and partiality. The British party do not like him on this account, but he keeps the safe side, as their loyalty is to be depended on. The idea of annexing Canada to the States is cherished by some few Americans. I copy the following from the 'Albany Daily Knickerbocker' of April 5th '54

"Annexing Canada: Mr Campbell of Ohio asked leave on Monday to introduce the following:- Resolved, that the President be requested to cause negotiations to be opened with the government of Great Britain with the view of ascertaining upon what conditions that government will consent to the annexation of the Canada to the United States of America". The proposition was voted down, Yeas 28, Nays 119.

I left the Gibraltar of the West on Saturday evening by the beautiful and commodious steamboat "John Munn". A poor horse was very nigh drowned just before starting. In leading him on board he became timid & trying to back off, his legs slipped off the gangway and in he went between the boat and dock. He was towed safely to shore in a rowboat, but could not by any means be induced to try again. A gent amused his fellow passengers at night by playing the piano and singing. I was badly fixed with a stateroom. I had first assigned to me one by the paddlebox, but the noise of the machinery was so unpleasant as to cause me to get it changed. I next got one with which I was satisfied but what was my consternation at night to find it hot as an oven. The fact was it was close to the boiler flues. Having a little cold upon me I thought a good perspiration would do me good. I gave it a trial, undressed and turned in. Like the iron floor however it got hotter, so in three hours, finding I was no salamander I dressed and taking my pillows into the saloon finished the night on a sofa very comfortably.

Arrived in Montreal on Sunday morning 4th and having been invited on Wednesday by Mr Warren of Notre Dame St to spend the day with him, I called there towards 10 o'clock and accompanied him to the English Cathedral, where I had the pleasure of hearing Bishop Fulford preach. I went with Mr W to dinner & in the afternoon accompanied by his wife, two children and a young lady, his sister-in-law, we had a ride round the mountain, returned to tea & after sitting awhile Mr W & I took a walk. I staid at the St Lawrence Hall this time and prefer it to either Donegana's or Montreal House. They had a severe fire the Sunday previous, by which they had about 40 rooms gutted. I was busy in Montreal till Tuesday evening when I left for New York. I took the rails to Rouse's Point (47 miles) which I reached at 7, went forward immediately by the steamboat "Canada" (a real floating palace) to Whitehall on Lake Champlain (125 miles). We had a thunderstorm and heavy rain during the night. Left the boat at 6 AM on Wednesday morning. Waited for the train at Whitehall Junction till 10 to 7 and then proceeded to Albany (79 miles) which we reached at $\frac{1}{2}$ p 10. I only took my ticket to here being wishful to come down the Hudson River, but arrived too late for the morning boat so had to finish my journey on the cars. I proceeded by the Hudson River Railroad (144 miles) at 11 AM and was in New York at $\frac{1}{4}$ to 5 PM. Thus was I brought safely back after an absence of nine weeks and a day in which I travelled independently of my peregrinations on foot a distance of 4332 miles, jumping from early spring yet scarcely summer, and back again to spring. I could not get the key of my office so after making some calls in New York and taking a salt bath at Fulton Ferry, I went up to Clinton St. where Miss Thompson's expressed themselves glad to see me and after passing the night with Milner and Sawyer who called upon us, I retired to sleep in my own little room. Thos. Littlewood is removed to Greenport, Long Island. He was ordained in the May Conference and the charge of a church there given to him. I am sorry he is gone so far away: about 100 miles from Brooklyn. Thursday 8th I have been busy arranging my new office at 212 Pearl St New York.

On making enquiry at the Post Office got quite a budget of letters which had missed being delivered on account of my removal. I have seen the letter carrier and hope to get all future letters right to hand. I had a treat at supper: strawberries and cream. I wonder if you have any ripe. There are also gooseberries and cherries in the market. There are few places to beat Brooklyn and New York, the one with its verdant shade and the other with its activity and excitement. Of the latter there has been an extra quantity lately in both places. Last Sunday there was quite a riot in B. between the Irish Catholics and the Protestants, the feelings of both parties being wrought up to an unsafe point by a street preacher. Thirty shots or more were interchanged. In New York the hurried trial and return of 3 fugitive slaves into bondage has caused a deal of unpleasantness. They were the brother and nephew of a Dr Pennington, a coloured gentleman much esteemed in Brooklyn. In Boston there have been serious riots from a similar cause.

The omnibuses in New York are becoming still more liberal. I can now go from Fulton Ferry to Crystal Palace, three miles for as many cents or 1½d. Isn't that cheap?

Sister Susan is a noble girl. I wish some worthy man would have sufficient discernment to ensure his happiness in connexion with her own. I will send you a paper now and then as the readiest means of giving the American views of the war question. I cannot believe that after my faithful service at a low rate that Mr S. will push Mr B. for the money. The "City of Glasgow" has not been heard of.

I am your affectionately,

Jno S. Webb

No. 24

18, Clinton St,

Brooklyn

July 28th '54

My dear Parents,

I am obliged by your kindness in writing to me, to answer you sooner than I intended, though no sooner than I ought, seeing that it is fully seven weeks since I last wrote. Please address in future to my office, 212, Pearl St. New York.

. . . .

I have not yet been present at any table moving, but in America many people's heads have experienced a strange sympathetic movement and grave learned men have written large tomes on that singular phenomenon and its train of concomitant impostures of rappings and mediums. Amongst the most eminent and sincere is Judge Edwards.

The tea making apparatus at the Botanical Gardens will not be quite so extensive as that at Sydenham Palace where I learned they are erecting a steam engine for the purpose.

. . . .

Father writes "No sun yet fair". There lies the difference between *our* climate and England. Here the sun knows how to shine and never thinks of going to bed till proper time, or wrapping himself up in the middle of the day. When he does go, he shuts up right away, leaving a beautiful smile on the clouds, which however soon follow him as if regretting his absence.

I have no commissions but Mr Brown's, should have no objections to good ones, but would require full sets of patterns of the goods you name. It is not quite certain that I shall come at Xmas. Mr B. is willing and I am wishful, but the expense is great. I shall be travelling a good deal between now and then and I shall be guided in my decision a good deal by the success of my journeys. Prices are so high that I do not expect much and I have already had many disappointments and countermands in consequence. I had much less anxiety when in Sheffield, and the charm of home to reconcile me to the monotony, but I rather think I should find the same life very irksome now.

I am still in New York but almost tired of it and shall probably be on the road in a week or ten days. I have not yet decided on my route. The last two months have been too hot for travelling with thermometer at 90°-104° in the shade, one does not feel equal to much exertion. Many at this time of the year leave the city to seek in the shady woods, the highland, or the breezy beach, a lower temperature, and relaxation from labour. I have I may say accidentally taken the same liberty but more of that anon. Gleason's Pictorial is much improved of late and contains much of interest, information and amusement. The woodcuts give you an idea of many places of note and it is my desire that you should have the work complete and bound. I have several numbers to send and any missing I shall be glad to supply. I take pleasure in its perusal, and it is enhanced by your partaking in the same.

The little street merchants have for some time included the air pistols Father described, amongst their articles of commerce and on 4th July they were much in request. I cannot think with you that it is a shame for rents to be raised in Sheffield. Good trade and high prices will naturally increase their value. Your house even in Newark, New Jersey where rents are much lower than N.Y. or Brooklyn would command a rent of $200 or over £40. I question if you can improve yourselves by removing, but you can obtain facts on the spot to judge by.

It is suspected of the King of Portugal that he covets the Spanish crown and is ingratiating himself with our Queen and the King of Belgium when he left England to visit as preparatory steps to obtaining it. You have had the sort of weather we wanted. Until the end of last week we had a dry time and everything in the garden was suffering. There would have been a Serious difference in the crops if it had continued longer and rain was hailed with delight by all.

Lord Elgin is a favourite only with the French Canadians whom he favours, the English and Scotch are down upon him, and on one occasion did not spare rotten eggs. Littlewood came out on speculation and had to seek employment on his arrival. He occupied two situations successively, the last was with Mr Cowlishaw. He was a local preacher in Sheffield and during his residence in New York & Brooklyn. He had a talent for the work and I rather think Dr Kennedy encouraged him to prosecute it. I received a kind note from him on the 19th inst. in which he says "It is no easy work I can assure you, a ministry life, and yet I would not exchange it, with all its hardships and discouragements, for the easiest and best business in the world." "Oh no I love the work dearly and more and more, the more I become engaged in it and accustomed to its exercise." He presses me to come and spend a Sunday with him, and if I can make it convenient to come out of New England by Stonington and Greenport, I shall avail myself of the invitation. My present office is not so large as the one in Gold Street. Please to let me know your rate of Insurance and if they can be effected and paid in N.Y.

Cold water is harmless and very acceptable. The heat is so great that its use increases perspiration instead of checking it. I am thankful that I perspire freely. Even when sitting still I am frequently obliged to use my handkerchief to my face and hands. Those who do not perspire suffer severely from heat. Habitual use of brandy takes away from its efficacy. I have had occasion to use it sometimes where the water does not suit strangers as at Montreal or Cincinatti. Apples are a failure this year in America as well as England and peaches are also a light crop.

On the 19th I went to Paterson & as I returned too late for supper & Milner came in about the same time, we went into the ice cream saloon next door and had it there. After that we crossed over to New York to call on the Cooks, Milner having promised to lend Miss C a book which she wished to take with her into the country next day. As I had intended visiting Albany having special business there, and she was going a little further up the river, I determined to accompany her so far. Next morning I was up at 4 o'clock and a little before 6 found me at Mr C's door but he had already taken her to the depot. I ran down Canal St. and jumped on one of the cars which are brought from the Central Depot in Chamber St. by horses and joined to the locomotive at 31st St. Arrived there I walked through the cars till I found her ladyship and Wallis her little brother. I took a ticket for Troy that I might see her safe there on to the Saratoga Cars. Arrived at Troy 150 miles at 11 am and Miss C pursuaded me to go forward to Schaghticoke assuring me a warm welcome from her friends. As the distance was only 14 miles I assented, intending to return to Albany the next day. Got to Mechanicville about 12, where Ishi and Mary Vernon met us with the wagon to take us across the River to S. By the bye, the ferry boat was a novelty to me. It consists of a strong flat bottomed boat with a rail at each side with posts on one side through which passes a rope stretching from bank to bank used by the boatman to pull it across. The Hudson is navigable only to Troy: I felt rather sheepish to be going without invitation, but the kind reception I met with set me at ease. We were glad to get in, for the day was awfully hot. I used an umbrella in the wagon but thought my limbs would be roasted. The family consists of Mr & Mrs Vernon, Miss Oakey who is Mrs V's sister, my old friend Miss Rebecca V, little Tommy, Miss Sarah, and the eldest son and daughter who escorted us. Mr V is a farmer with some 300 acres of land lying along the river some of it wooded. The house is plank, of no pretension to beauty but pleasant and convenient. In the afternoon we had some quiet games in the house and partook of cherries fresh from the trees. At night I rowed the four young ladies on the river, and the boys with a friend who was also visiting at the house, by name Fred Lewis, and Sarah the youngest daughter had a boat to themselves. After that we all had a pleasant walk, Ishi having also joined us. On Friday morning my new friends would not hear of my leaving so soon, so while the ladies attended to their household duties Miss C and Sarah & I went down to the shady banks of the river and roamed about till we quite lost Sarah. Miss C and I then had it all to ourselves, and enjoyed the fresh air, shade, and retirement as only the denizens of a busy city can. Three squirrels bounded by us on their gambols. After dinner we all went into the woods. I was thankful to be there for this was the hottest day we have had this season. At night we rowed across the river and strolled about Mechanicville. On Saturday 22nd after Miss Mary and I had got some worms for bait all we boys and girls went to the river to fish. Fred caught a bass directly his line got into the water and so did I. He afterwards caught three more and Miss Mary caught an eel after which the fish would not bite. Very ungrateful conduct indeed considering what trouble we took to feed them. After dinner I went to the Depot & waited 2 hours. The train did not come, so back I tramped to Mr V's. Oh! how they did laugh when they saw me, but not near so much then as a little later. Not expecting to be more than a day away I had not brought a shred of baggage, during the three days I had rolled about on the grass and among the trees till I was a real punky. You may conceive the effect of this when I further tell you that I was dressed in a white coat and vest, very light linen pants and light silk necktie. Well, says Mrs V, when people have no change of linen, they generally go to bed while it is washed, but I wont serve you so. I was therefore invested in a complete suit and mine consigned to the washtub. Did they not laugh when I introduced myself as my cousin. On Sunday morning the wagon was brought out to take us to church about 2½ miles off, same side of the river. Ishi drove us with a span of horses, Miss C, Mary, Rebecca, Sarah, Tommy, Fred, Wallis & myself making the party. Passed Mr Knickerbocker's house where Washington Irving wrote the work bearing that name. I met Mr K's son after service, the same I was introduced to at Mr Cook's. Ishi is a mischievous rogue and going through the woods, drove over every stump and into every rut he could find. We did not go out after dinner. It was too hot for exertion. Left Mr V's house on Monday morning with the real determination to go to Albany. Met Mr V in the fields, who pointing to a heavy thundercloud, told me if I ventured I should be wet through in a few minutes and sure enough we had to run for it. Heavier rain I think I never saw. There was some more clapping and laughing to see the bad money.[*] After dinner I again essayed to go but Mr V would not hear of it, and persuaded me to wait till morning, lest I should again be disappointed. We then walked over the farm to observe the crops and cattle. I tried to catch a little black snake which crossed my path but it was too quick for me. Ishi and Fred were out all day in true Sportsman style, wading in the water. They caught a few black bass which we had to breakfast next morning. Fred also caught a toothache which was not so good. I saw a little humming bird in the garden. At night we had a fine time in the house and almost succeeded in turning the house out of the windows, dancing and games of all kinds, finishing up with raspberry vinegar and water, a favourite beverage, for a nightcap. I saw a great number of hornets here, indeed they had three nests in sight, just outside the windows. I left my very kind friends on Tuesday morning and proceeded to Albany. I did my business and some little commissions for Mr V and left for N.Y. at $\frac{1}{2}$ p 7 pm in the noble steamboat "Isaac Newton" one of the best in America. This is the first time I have sailed down the Hudson. The night was cloudy with lightning, but the breeze was quite warm and few chose to stay in the magnificent Gothic saloon. I arrived at N.Y. at 6 am. When I got over to Brooklyn at night, all were glad to see me, for they had become quite anxious, and M told me that Miss Thompson had even suggested the propriety of making some enquiries or advertising for information.

Met Miss Vale at supper and took her home to Williamsburg where I was asked to call again. She is a pleasant lively girl with more good sense than many of her sex, and I really enjoyed her society. Thursday night I walked down to my washerwoman to give her directions about my clothes, that I might have all ready for my journey. Since my return I have paid her 5/- a doz York money equal to 2/6 sterling. The weather has not been quite so hot the last day or two. New Orleans which was so scourged

[*] nowadays "bad penny"

with the yellow fever last year is one of the healthiest cities in the Union at the present time.

With much love, Believe me dear father and mother
to be your affectionate dutiful son,
Jno S. Webb

P.S. I cannot help thinking I have done wrong in taking this pleasure trip but I relate simple facts and if I have erred you must reprove me.

No 25 omitted
No. 26

Cincinatti,
Ohio
Oct 21st 1854

Very dear Parents,

I have before me your joint letter of 7th Sept. received 22nd Sept. It gave me much pleasure to know that dear Mother realised her desire to visit Aughton and dear Father was busy.

That there is a time to weep and a time to be joyful is illustrated in Mr Moulson's family, by the death of one son and marriage of the other. The supposition of pieces of the wreck of the "City of Glasgow" steamer being seen, reminds me of news lately received here of the discovery of the remains of Capt. Franklin and his party who were frozen to death near the mouth of the Fox River.

Thanks dear Father for your good advice. I will profit by it if I have the opportunity. I only wish I may be *able* to walk the deck. On my outward trip I found my limbs quite unmanageable and vexed as I was at my rolling unsteady gait, many a time did I laugh at my drunkard-like movements.

Your remarkable fine weather has extended to us and produced lamentable results. Speaking of corn, I might say to you as Mr Fraser once said to me when looking together on a field of wheat that isn't corn. "By corn we Americans understand the produce of that plant between the thriving rows of which even horses are hid from sight and which I have heard called "the Pocohontas of grain". "The Indian Empress among cereals". The crops in Ohio and parts of Pennsylvania have been light. In the more western states as Illinois, Wisconsin etc they have been good.

I left Rochester on 10th at 4 pm for Lockport, 56 miles, a spreading town only 20 miles from Niagara Falls. Arrived 7 pm and put up at an excellent hotel called the Tremont. A number of ladies were performing on saxe horns[*] in one of the public rooms of the town but though such a novelty I did not feel in humour to hear them. Left Lockport for Buffalo next morning at 11. 25½ m. Arrived at 1.0 pm and put up at American Hotel. Left for Cleveland on Thurs. morning at 7½ o'clock 183 miles, arrived at 2½ pm and put up at American Hotel. Here at dinner I tasted a new dish, fricaséed squirrel and found it rich and delicate. Left for Pittsburgh on 13th by rails all the way, 139 miles at 2.50 pm, arrived at 9.50 and put up at Monongahela House. Just such weather as last time, dull and showery, and enshrouding this dirty disagreeable city like the silk worm in a pall of its own making. While in Pittsburgh I anxiously watched the river or rather its ghost for there was precious little body in it. But the daily assurance that a boat might go down on the morrow was not verified. The day before it only rose one inch and when ready to go there was only 19 inches water in the channel. On Tuesday morning there being no alternative I took my seat in the stage for Wheeling, 60 miles, at 6 o'clock. I really enjoyed the journey the country through which we passed being very hilly and picturesque and the passengers pleasant and affable. We had a comfortable dinner at Washington Pa, and in the afternoon entered the Old Dominion id. est. Virginia called by the former name on account of its loyal fidelity to the banished king of England. Arrived at Wheeling at 5½ pm and billetted myself at the Sprigg House. At tea I noticed at another table a number of Indians and on making enquiries learned that they were going to exhibit some of their customs. I determined to see them and found myself at near 8 pm. in a tent roughly furnished with graduated benches all full, about 500 people present. Oceala the chief came forward and explained that he and his companions

[*] first introduced in 1845

107

were about to show the various dances etc. of Indians in an uncivilised state. How foolish and ignorant they were he illustrated by an anecdote. When the first steamboat appeared at Mackinaws on Lake Huron the natives hastened in their canoes to see it and by degrees were induced to go on board; while stopping the engineer let off the steam on hearing which they all plunged into the water and told their tribe that the sailors had the evil spirit in a box, that he carried the ship on his back and pushed it along with his claws (the paddle wheels) but when he began to blow his nose they thought it time to be off. Oceala also told us that his party were of the Calapooah Indians of N. California, that they were brought to this part of the country by the missionary for the express purpose of obtaining an education and then would return to do their people good. During the evening they showed their funeral ceremony at the death of a Chief, then spy dances, war, greencorn, rattlesnake, courting and death dances, all accompanied by the monotonous drum rattle and chaunt of the Indians.

On 18th I left Wheeling at 4 pm for Columbus. I travelled all night by coach to Cambridge 50 miles. We were very much crowded having 8 men, 2 women and 5 children inside, and 4 men outside besides the driver and only four horses. To ensure an inside place I took a little girl 6 years old on my knee and nursed her all the way. Fortunately on this and the former occasion I was free from any feeling of coach sickness, which from the time I rode in a wagon to Dronfield* I have generally experienced. The poor horses on this road, having, since the drying up of the rivers to take the Cincinatti passengers as well as those for central Ohio, are almost used up. After finishing their stage of ten miles, they scarcely reach the stable before another coach takes them away. Our progress was therefore what poor Wm. Axe used to call "a caution to a snail". Though we stayed nowhere for supper it was 5½ next morning before we reached Cambridge. The poor outsiders complained that they had to walk about half way and were all but iced. I do not wonder for a sharper morning I have not felt. From thence we went by rails to Columbus 85 miles. Passed through Newark where the state capital Fair was being held. At Zanesville 26 miles this side we changed cars, and so great was the crowd going thither that we were glad of standing room. Cattle vans were filled with bipeds,

* 10 miles from Sheffield

looking like so many felons going to be transported. Arrived at Columbus at ½ p 10, put up at the Neil House and never felt so glad as when dinner was announced, having had nothing but an apple and 2 little ginger cakes for 24 hours. This is the seat of government for Ohio and is a fine city of 25,000 inhabitants with broad streets and numerous manufactories. Its chief boast is the Capitol or State House, a massive structure of white stone, not yet completed. Left for Dayton on 20th at 10 am. by rail road 73 miles and arrived there at 2 pm. put up at the Phoenix Hotel. The country for many miles presents alternately forests and farms, the latter well cultivated and generally productive with but few hills. Dayton has 20,000 and is but little inferior to Columbus. This morning I started at 7½ am. by rail to Cincinatti 60 miles arrived about 11 am. and put up at the Spencer House. I regret to say that business is very dull and the merchants are determined under the circumstances to give no orders. The want of trade is not the least lamentable feature. The State Legislation by improper measures, undue interference and exorbitant taxation of the Banks, have driven capitalists to withdraw and a want of confidence is added to scarcity of money. Banks in the West are breaking in all directions and runs upon good banks are trying them to the utmost. I shall not be surprised at a panic ensuing. The present season will be one of great suffering to labourers and mechanics. Many of the railroads in operation are stopped for want of funds, and in one factory alone in Columbus 150 hands are to be discharged out of 250. I have determined to go no further, but proceed direct from here to Detroit and into Canada. This is a sad falling off from last year's prosperity, God grant it may not come to the worst. Apropos of Canada a gigantic structure across the St. Lawrence was commenced last July near Montreal and already one of the piers to support the Victoria iron bridge of 2 miles in length is several feet above water. This unparalleled undertaking is to be finished in 1858 and is to form an unbroken line of railways between the two countries. This is anexation indeed. Let the Thames Tunnel bury itself in its slime and darkness.

But I must conclude or this will miss the mail.

With much love believe me my dear Father and Mother

your affectionate son

Jno S. Webb

(I must interrupt the 1853 letters to quote from one written to Ethel in 1897)

In Dec. 1854 when as no business could be done at that season, I decided to have a run over to England. My absence from "the old folks at home" for 1¾ years having made me hungry to see them again. I arrived in Liverpool on Xmas Eve and could only get on as far as Manchester. On reaching Sheffield my dear father met me at the Station. As I had grown a beard in the meantime he had to look hard at me and ask "Is that you, John?" I think I see him now, how delighted he was to see his boy again. When we got home, had I not as warm a welcome from dear mother and Susan; aye, and still another my old nurse Mary Buxton, who lived with us as domestic in Furnival St. in my very early days, and whose fingers I used to lick after she had been clearing out the pudding dish! A, my son, (she usually called me so) I am glad to see thee; I've been dreaming about you that you were made governor of the Bank of England; I wish it may come true. Her husband was a spring knife cutler and the good old soul had brought me a knife as a welcome home present. I had been only a day or two at home when my sister Susan was anxious to know if I had made any

Aughton Vicarage

110

attachment. She was very glad I had not, and she spoke very highly of her friend Miss Krauss, and said she was sure she would make me a good wife. I was rather impressed, and said I might think about it if I found such a jewel in a suitable casket. She then showed me a portrait of her and after further talk she promised to arrange a visit to our brother George and invite Miss Krauss to meet her there to spend a few days. Your aunt Sarah was let into the plot and played her part "con amore" by sending Miss Krauss a pressing invitation. Our plans had well nigh been defeated through Miss K's affectionate solicitude for her mother who was ill. Another letter still more pressing was sent in sister Susan's name and Mrs K. being a little better Miss K. consented to join Susan at Aughton. I think it is due both to myself and the young lady I have mentioned to make some apology for the undue haste as it might be called with which we took possession of each other's affections. We had both, through the same trusted medium, been pre-impressed in each other's favour and we seemed to meet as old acquaintances rather than as strangers. From our first meeting (Jan 6th '55) in the dining room at Aughton Vicarage I felt as if I should have no need to go further in search. I did not stay all the time of Miss K's visit, but I returned to Aughton before she left and on our return to our homes accompanied her to Normanton, where our ways diverted. This was an eventful journey. We had scarcely entered the train at Bubwith, the nearest station to Aughton, than I asked her to be my wife, and she did not refuse, only stipulating that her parents consent should be got before I was to consider it an engagement. This happened only eleven days (Jan 17) after we had first seen one another. Oh happy day! Oh happy choice! for this great gift of a loving faithful heart I still thank God daily after two and forty years. A short time after, I went to Manchester to interview Father and Mother Krauss. Dear simple souls, all they thought of was their Mary Hannah's happiness, and trusting me to secure *that* they asked no questions of ways and means. And so our short courtship went on. The Krauss family were much disturbed on learning that I purposed to take Mary Hannah in a short time to America but they got reconciled to it as their liking for me increased. As for my own folks it was a marvel to me how affectionately they all took to my lady love. As M.H. was in Manchester, I suppose getting ready, and I was engaged in Sheffield we had little opportunity of seeing one another in the interval; but we both kept the postman busy. I indulged in the holiday privilege of rising late, but my dear mother had the whip hand of me. Her voice would soon make me stir quickly with "John, there's a letter for you from Miss Krauss; you can't have it till you come down". What a powerful magnet it was! But the time of waiting was short. The wedding took place (March 7th) exactly seven weeks from our engagement and fortunately the proverb "Marry in haste, repent at leisure", though often true, was not so in our case. We were married from Park Street at Manchester Cathedral by my dear brother George, and had a merry party at breakfast. In the after part of the day after we were seen off on our honeymoon, there was a *great* stir, carpets up, dancing etc. We left for America three weeks later.

Ever your affectionate father

John S. Webb

P.S. That I may avoid the charge of imprudence in so hastily engaging myself to marry a young lady on so short an acquaintance, I desire to add particulars of the way in which it was brought about. Between August 1852 and Dec. 1853 my dear sister Susannah was engaged in teaching at a boarding school called Torkington, kept by the Misses Hughes. Miss Krauss was also there, and my sister became much attached to her, as you may learn from the following quotations out of letters addressed to me. In Jan^y, 1853 she wrote "Would that you could have seen dear Mary Hannah, young, pious, amiable, all that you could wish, but I will not say more; if not for you, for some blessed mortal she will be one of these whose price is above rubies." It seemed to be a case of love at first sight, for she wrote on Aug. 20th 1852 "Miss Krauss, my fellow assistant is a sweet amiable girl (23) and makes my situation more agreeable than it would otherwise be". Also on Dec. 8th "She is the dearest girl I ever knew". Could I hesitate after such testimony from a trusted sister?

No 14

Glasgow

Feb 22nd 1897

My dear Ethel,

Our honeymoon trip (to Huddersfield and York) was a short one, for we wished to see as much of our dear ones as we could before our departure to America. One important matter I was endeavouring to arrange, viz., to

Aughton Church

find a home which would afford us a comfortable reception on our arrival in the States. There was no room for us in the boarding houses in Brooklyn wherein I had been an inmate. Having left the country in complete unconsciousness of the happiness in store for me, I had made no enquiries for necessary accommodation on the spot. But this difficulty was happily solved. I had some intimate acquaintances in Newark N.J., a Mr Crookes and his two sisters, Miss Marshalls, Sheffield people, who were willing to receive us. I paid ten dollars a week, and for several months we had a comfortable home with them. It was a good thing to have pleasant people for company for M.H. when I was away travelling, and even through the day when I was in New York. Very soon after settling ourselves I had to take a journey of eight weeks!

Marriage Certificate

John S. Webb

with

Mary Hannah Krauss.

Manchester.
March 7th 1855

I hereby certify that John Stubbins Webb, and Mary Hannah Krauss were this day married by me in the Cathedral Church of Manchester, in the presence of (among other Witnesses) the following:—

John Krauss Senior
Thomas Carter
Elizabeth Adelaide Krauss.
Susannah Webb.

} Witnesses.

Geo. M. Webb,
Vicar of Aughton.
York.

Manchester
March 7th 1855

Marriage certificate

114

J.S.W. & M.H.W. sailed on Sat. March 31st, 1855.

MHW on board "The America" Royal Mail
April 9th 1855, 11.20 am. (Monday)

My very dear Parents,

My first attempt at letter writing on shipboard is to be devoted to you. I have just heard that there is a probability of our being able to post letters when we touch Halifax which we expect to do in the course of 3 or 4 days by which means you would receive intelligence of us some days earlier than you anticipated which I know will give you pleasure. We are at present enveloped in a fog which prevents going on deck so I am very glad to amuse myself so pleasantly as in talking with you. We have had in general very favourable weather, tho' the first days of last week were very rough and nearly everybody was ill. I was not able to leave my berth after Saturday night until Thursday when I spent a few hours in the ladies' saloon (where I am sitting at this moment) but Friday, Saturday (7th) and yesterday I enjoyed many hours on deck as the weather was very bright and pleasant. I have been under the surgeon's care since Wednesday for I have suffered very much, in addition to the seasickness, from an immense boil on my chin, which has been poulticed incessantly since Tuesday & has not yet disappeared, but I am thankful to say that I expect this will be the last day they will be required. I have not taken one meal in the saloon since the first day we came on board, but this room is a very pleasant one and I am not at all sorry to escape from the lengthy repasts in the Saloon. The hours for meals are Breakfast at 8½ am, Lunch at 12, Dinner at 4: (it usually lasts until 5½) and tea at 7½. Supper about 9, I think. There is a great variety in the viands at every meal, but I have not yet been able to enjoy them. However I think both dear John and myself have now recovered from seasickness and shall henceforth do justice to the provisions. The stewardess is a very kind agreeable person, we called her "Scotchie" until we knew her name, which however soon showed us that we were not mistaken in her nationality for it is no other than Macbeth. She has already crossed the Atlantic 117 times!!

There are 116 passengers on board and 100 hands employed in various capacities on the vessel. There are seven cooks besides a butcher and baker, & I should imagine there is not much leisure for any of them as

115

there is a constant succession of meals going on. No sooner has one taken place at one end of the vessel than another comes on at the other.

We had a very nice service yesterday in the Saloon. The Surgeon read prayers, and there was a minister of the Scotch Free Church on board who gave us a very good sermon. Some of the sailors were present and were very orderly and attentive. They looked so nice in their dark blue uniforms. There are many Scotchmen on board and some French Canadians, some Portuguese and Germans. They are a very well-behaved set of people, and there is much good feeling amongst them all (apparently) which makes it very pleasant. Many, perhaps the majority are destined for Canada.

I have only made acquaintance with a few of the ladies, there is a young lady sitting beside me just now, employed like myself in writing home who has been to California, whither she is going again now, to Australia, New Zealand, and the United States, and she came from Dublin the day before the vessel started, and she is only 18 years old. She is travelling quite alone but has found some good friends among the ladies, she is very lively & agreeable.

Both John and I thought of you all very much yesterday, & I found great enjoyment both then and on Good Friday in reading the sweet hymns from the book dear Father gave us before parting, and I will just assure him now that he could not have given me a more acceptable present than that.

. . . .

Tuesday April 10th. I am happy to tell you that I have at last got rid of the poultices and now feel quite well. I must also tell you what a dear kind attentive nurse I have had in my illness. Dear John has made all the poultices (they were linseed meal) and applied them himself changing them every four hours, so you may imagine he has felt he has got a new charge in his wife, but he seems to think it only a pleasure to do anything for me. The doctor has ordered me porter and wine as he thinks me not strong, but I know my weakness only proceeded from seasickness & now I am all right again. I do not like writing so much about myself, but I think you will wish to have all particulars.

We are now on the banks of Newfoundland. The fog did not last all day yesterday, & in spite of it we had a better day's run than any we have yet made (220 miles). We usually go about 9 miles per hour. We feel the cold today more than we have ever done before (indeed some days have been quite warm) I suppose because we are approaching the North. I have been very much impressed by the apparently small dimension of the horizon, it has a very curious appearance when the sky is clear, we seem to be as it were on the top of a hill whose summit is completely round and flat only sloping downwards at the edges but the blue sky seems so far beyond that we appear to be on the centre of an immense dome. Then however fast we travel we never seem to be any nearer one side of the horizon or further from the other. I have not seen a single ship since Saturday week though we passed several last week; on Thursday there were three in sight, nor had I the pleasure of once seeing the moon when evenings were illuminated by its beams.

Thursday morning. We had a very favourable wind all day yesterday and made more progress than we have ever done before (239 miles), and as we expect to be at Halifax some time today, I must draw my letter to a close. John intends to leave his open that you may read it before sending it to Sheffield, as it contains more statistics than mine. We are indulging the hope that you will receive them next Sunday week, and I should dearly love to be a witness of the pleasure which I flatter myself the receipt of them will give. However I can be with you in spirit, as indeed I am, times without number. Our fellow passengers as well as ourselves seem now perfectly restored to health, and our appetites are amazingly good.

We hope to be in Boston sometime on Saturday . . . . My boil has cost dear John £1, a very dear one, was it not?

I know you will excuse the bad writing as you are aware of the circumstances in which I wrote.

Again accept my best love and believe me,
My dear Parents,
Your very affectionate daughter,
Mary Hannah.

JSW

April 12th 1855

P.S. On Tuesday I saw about 8 vessels and yesterday two. I have just had an accident with my desk and upset the ink & you see my letter has not escaped the catastrophe so I must again beg you to excuse defects.

P.S. Please do not lose a post in sending my letter to Sheffield. I hope John & Joe enjoyed themselves after our departure. I shall not soon forget them as they stood on the receding tug. I am thankful that dear M.H. was able to part from all she had held dear with such firmness. It is a pleasure to me to do all I can to make up the loss, & I hope in the consciousness of such endeavour, you may comfort yourselves in our absence.

With love to all, I am

Your Affe. son,

Stubbins

JSW   Steamship "America" Atlantic Ocean

April 10th 1855

My dear Parents,

As we may possibly be in time at Halifax to send letters by the steamer which leaves Boston tomorrow & calls at the former place on the way to L'pool we, that is my wife and I, wish to be ready to profit by the opportunity to allay your anxiety on our account at the earliest possible date. We have hitherto had a tolerable passage, that is the sea has been calm & the wind at times on our larboard quarter so as to permit the use of the sails occasionally, but our ship is a slowcoach and one day only made 149 miles & about 10 knots an hour is the greatest speed we have ever reached. To do her justice I must state that she is heavily freighted and her engines only 640 horse power.

We have a great number of passengers, chiefly first class altogether 146, the officers & men about 100 total 246 souls. The amount received for passengers is about £3,200,* which with the charge for freight & the government allowance for carrying the mail will make the gross receipts £8000 or £9000 for this trip. The expenses are great. The amount of coals

---

* possibly thus: 80 at £26 £2080 ; 36 at £20 £720; 30 at £14 £420; Total £3200

consumed per day not less than 50 tons the provisions are liberal and bill of fare varied. A great drawback to the enjoyment of the good things prepared for us is the abominable seasickness from which both MH & I have suffered considerably, she has I think had less of it than myself. She has had an obstinate boil on her chin which made the surgeon's assistance necessary. I am glad to say that after some days poulticing I have had the satisfaction of putting some court plaster on this morning with a view to its being finally healed. I have been picking up my crumbs this last day or two to make up for lost time, and I hope that now MH is freed from her bandages, she will be with me at dinner today, that I may take care of her myself and encourage her by my example. She has hitherto had her meals in bed or in the ladies' saloon & as she appeared to be an invalid I am afraid they treated her as such.

We have a mixture of all kinds of people on board: English, French, Scotch, Spanish, Portuguese, Americans, Canadians, Californians, New Brunswickers, etc. etc. a feeling of harmony and good fellowship pervades the whole. Last Sunday MH & I attended Divine Service in the Saloon. A number of sailors were present & the large room was quite full. The surgeon read prayers & a minister of the free Church preached a good sermon. His topics were humility & obedience in accordance with our great example. The people are employed whilst I write, in reading, writing, talking, whist & drafts & some are walking vigorously on the main deck overhead to digest their breakfasts & promote circulation this cold morning. So are the days spent a great deal of time being also given to meals. Dinner occupies usually an hour & a half.

The distance from L'pool to Halifax is 2450 miles & from Halifax to Boston 385 miles, being rather more than 200 miles less than the route to New York. We have hopes of being in Boston on Saturday. But I must conclude that I may take MH a walk on deck.

Apr.	3	Lat.		Long.			distance	148
	4	"	51.1	"	21.18		"	149
	5	"	–	"	–		"	169
	6	"	50.12	"	30.44		"	194
	7	"	49.34	"	35.54		"	213
	8	"	47	"	40.14		"	211

9	" –	" –	" 224
10	" 44.51	" 50°W at 12 noon	" 218
11	" 44.46	" 55.32 " " "	" 239
12	" 44.46	" 62° " " "	" 270

JSW   April 12 1855

My Dear Parents,

Having just had breakfast MH & I have sat down to finish our letters as we expect to reach Halifax at 6. o'clock this evening. How glad we are in the prospect of seeing land after being surrounded by the wild wilderness of the waters. And yet the last two or three days we have been very comfortable & happy having overcome the horrible feeling of seasickness & become reconciled to the continual motion of the vessel. The great difficulty is to pass the time, as the novel circumstances by which we are surrounded make it impossible to apply the mind to one object for long together. Take a day's experience, for example. At eight o'clock the first bell rings for us to rise. We accordingly turn out taking especial care in doing so, lest we should roll out too quickly to the detriment of our arms neck or limbs. We have a walking monument on board, who, by such precipitation, has been obliged to have one arm in a sling for several days. From him we take warning. To proceed, at $8\frac{1}{2}$ the bell rings again, for breakfast, which usually lasts until about 10. At 12 another bell announces lunch: at $\frac{1}{2}$ p 3 the preparatory bell and at 4 for dinner, which with its courses of soup, fish, fowl, flesh, pastry & dessert last about $1\frac{1}{2}$ hours, at $7\frac{1}{2}$ we are again summoned to tea. We have no formal supper but may order individually anything we want. The intervals are filled up in the manner already mentioned & so the days go. "We eat & drink & sleep & then" "We eat & drink & sleep again". I shall have to make up for all this idleness when I get ashore. Indeed so multitudinous are my engagements that I shall not know where to begin. I shall feel glad to be at work again *in my dear America* away from the smoke cloud & fog of old England & especially – but I say no more for fear of offending.

The weather is favourable & as the ship is lighter we speed better on our way. The "America" is, I am told, only 1800 tons burthen so that the consumption of coals & provisions to the amount of 600 tons makes a great difference to her. We have seen but little by the way until the day before yesterday when about 10 ships were observed.

Whilst we are proceeding so well, how is it with you my dear Parents? You have often been in my thoughts and I have wondered how you were and if you made yourselves miserable with groundless fears on our account. I shall be pleased to know when you get our letters. M.H. & I still love each other and have agreed to continue the honeymoon to the end of the year. We may contrive to keep off quarreling and fighting a little longer even.

I remain, as ever,

Yours most affectionately

John.

The letters of M.H.W. of which there were more, have been very serverely cut because she wrote less of matters of general interest than J.S.W.

MHW

102 Orchard St

Newark

Monday May 14/55

Mr & Mrs Webb

My very dear Father & Mother,

We were very much pleased to receive the first letter from Sheffd. last week. Nothing of importance has occurred since I wrote last week except that John has been obliged to defer his Canada journey for a short time, so that I have not been deprived of the pleasure of his company as I expected. He hopes to set off in a day or two, and then I am to be a "widow" for 5 weeks! & when our happiness depends so much on each other you may be sure the separation is not a pleasant prospect to either of us; however it is one of the things that must be & therefore it is best to meet it cheerfully & to make ourselves as happy as we can under the circumstances. There will be the joy of anticipating a reunion and we shall be all the more precious to each other when we do meet again, though I rather doubt the possibility of our loving each other more than we do now. I am afraid we shall not be considered as legal claimants for the "flitch of bacon" * as we are not living in England, else I have no fear that we should be entitled to it.

We do very often think of you all & should be quite as happy to join you at the social evening meal, as you would be to have our company; but we cannot have all we wish for in this world, so we try to be contented.

The weather now is very fine & pleasant. All nature is springing into life & beauty. The fruit trees make a fine show of bloom especially the peaches & cherry. Miss Marshall & I sowed a number of seeds last Saturday but one, viz. lettuce, radishes, mustard & cress, parsley & onions, and they are all come up but the two latter. Mr Littlewood came for a short visit on Friday & Mr Sawyer joined him on Saturday. They both stayed until this morning. The former is going to Danbury to a conference where he has to pass an examination previous to his ordination, which made him feel rather nervous; he preached twice yesterday. In the morning he went into Church with Mr Crookes without any expectation of being called on to preach. He made a good sermon but I believe that of the evening was better, tho' I did not hear it as dear John & I went to the Episcopal church where we heard a very inferior sermon, the chief recommendation of which was its brevity, it only lasted a quarter of an hour. John went to Bridgeport last Thursday & stayed until Friday evening. He had a pleasant journey, the country is looking so beautiful. We have captured a mosquito this morning, the first of the season, but they do not begin to bite at present, at least not in the houses until nearer July.

We are both, I am thankful to say, quite well & happy. We have a very comfortable house here, & John's only objection to Newark is so far from New York that we cannot go over to any of the meetings etc as he could from Brooklyn. We are both grieved to find such a defective ministry in the Episcopalian Church as it prevents our attending it with any pleasure or profit.

I can fancy the country around Sheffield looking very lovely now & tho' I have not seen it clothed with verdure, I do believe it is very beautiful & I hope to see it for myself someday. I think dear Susan's walks in an evening must be very pleasant now. I suppose she is still very fully employed.

---

* *A side or flitch of bacon is awarded annually still at Dunmow, Essex to the couple whose marriage proves to have been the happiest among the contestants. T.B.D.*

It is six weeks last Saturday since we left our native land and I can scarcely believe that I have only been here a little more than three weeks, it appears more like three months or even six. I feel quite at home now. Accept, my dear Father and Mother, much fond love, and give a portion to each of the family circle & believe me ever

Your very affece. daughter

Mary Hannah Webb

MHW to Susan No 2

111 Orchard St

Newark

New Jersey

May 29th 1855

My precious sister & friend,

I cannot tell you how anxiously I have looked for a letter from you for some weeks past, but as I have not yet received one I write to you a few lines to show you that I do not attribute your silence to any diminution of affection on your part, but to some error in the dispatch of letters. We have had only one letter from all our Sheffield & Aughton friends, & at least 10 or a dozen from Manchester. John had a letter from Mr Brown yesterday which was written in Liverpool where Mr B was staying. I have often heard of you, dear Susan, from Manchester & by the last account I was sorry to find that you were not well; I hope you are better now: you must go to Aughton during the holidays to recruit & no doubt you will meet friends there who will cheer you up. Do you and my dear brother John continue your correspondence? How does it progress? John & I will join you in imagination if you go to Aughton. Oh! that we could do so in reality! I do so long to see you all at times! I should be very unhappy if dear John did not love me so tenderly: but he is too good & kind for me to allow myself to be discontented.

He is now away from home on his Canadian journey, he intends (D.V.) to return about the 22nd of June. He set off last Wednesday but one, but was obliged to return to New York the following Saturday and business detained him here the whole week, so that he only started again yesterday. He ought to have someone to help him, he is so often wanted in two places at once, & when he goes on his journey of course his office must be closed.

The country about here, or rather the vegetation looks very beautiful now there are some roses in bloom & many more in bud, and the trees are completely covered with their spring foliage. On Saturday afternoon Mr Crookes & his sisters & John & I went over to Brooklyn & thence by cars to Greenwood where we spent between two and three hours in the cemetry [sic]. It is indeed a most beautiful place: although I had heard most charming descriptions of it previous to going, it far surpassed my anticipations. I remember you reading me an account of it from one of dear John's letters, when we were at Torkington together, but little thought then that I should see it one day myself. The trees & flowering shrubs are truly beautiful & the graves are planted with many choice flowers. The monuments, too, are very splendid – some very interesting. We stayed some time in that portion which is devoted to the little children's graves & it was most interesting to see the toys etc. which are placed in glass cases on many of the graves and some are planted with flowers. . . . .

The daisies we brought from Aughton are now in flower & I assure you they are quite a treasure. An old lady in this city who left England about 30 years since has bespoken one. There are many English people here. I hope you will like the likeness we are sending by this steamer.

Please give my love to Mary Ann, also to dear Father & Mother.

Your fondly loving sister,

Mary Hannah

MHW No 3

111 Orchard St

Newark

Tuesday June 12th 1855

Mr & Mrs Webb

My dear Father and Mother,

Since I began to write my letters for tomorrow's mail, I have learned that Mr Sawyer has kindly offered to convey any letters I may have to send to England as he is going (D.V.) to set sail for his native land in the 'Pacific' tomorrow, with his bride – they are to be married today.

I had a letter from dear John yesterday from Brantford C.W. dated June 6th from it I fear that he will not be home before next Friday week – I do feel the separation very much, but I know it cannot be avoided, so I endeavour to make myself as happy as possible. Miss Marshalls & Mr Crooke are very kind – they try not to let me feel lonely. We have called on many pleasant people since I came here, & I have no doubt I shall soon have some nice friends, but you know there is none of the social going out to tea that we are accustomed to in dear Old England, the visiting is mostly calls made either in the afternoon or after supper. I have not taken one meal out of this house except when I have been in New York. John has found trade here very dull but it is only what he expected: he says it will be some time before confidence is restored: he has been informed of the proposed change in Mr B's affairs but matters are not all arranged yet. It is to take place on the 1st July.

Strawberries are plentiful now in the market, but they arc very small. I had the pleasure of gathering a few myself in the garden of an English friend of the Marshalls last Monday week. Our garden has produced abundance of radishes & mustard & cress also the lettuce & parsley are in a progressive state. I wish you could just see the profusion of roses now in bloom in Newark, they present in some places a complete sheet of flowers covering half the side of a house, they are red, yellow, pink & a few white.

I have been reading this week a new book by the Rev. Henry Ward Beecher (one of Mrs Stowe's brothers) it is entitled "Star Papers" or "Experience of Art & Nature". They are very interesting. I met with one article that pleased me so much that I intend copying a portion of it to send to George because I think it will suit his ideas, you will have an opportunity of reading it. I think you will like it too.

If Susan were to see dear John's letters to me I think she would not say "the honeymoon was over" I think each one is more affectionate than its predecessor. I am sure no love letters were ever sweeter. I don't think there is much fear of our quarreling this year. I shall never be unhappy while he loves me so tenderly, though I cannot say "I like America".

It is said in New York papers that Barnum realized above $17,300 by the five days of his Baby Show last week, he kept it open longer than at first proposed, & the average attendance each day was between 10,000

& 12,000 persons. Don't you think he could afford to give away $1,100 in premiums at that rate?

I hope you are all quite well. I am better now than I have been since I left England. Accept my very dear love & give a portion to each member of the family circle, also remember me kindly to all friends.

I remain, My dear Parents,
Yours most affectionately,
Mary Hannah Webb

JSW   212 Pearl St
No 29   New York
(nos. 27 & 28 are missing)

Sept 11th/55

My dear Parents,

I must have several letters of yours unanswered but as they are at home in Newark you must excuse my reference to them and as my dear M.H. has noticed them in hers, nothing perhaps remains for me but to thank you for every rememberance of the absent and good wishes for their welfare. The last week I spent in the City of Brotherly Love (Ph^a) & the Monumental City (Balt^e) leaving home on the Tuesday morning & returning on Saturday night. The weather being fine & not too hot was exceedingly pleasant. The country looks well, though the freshness of spring & the fullness of summer is giving way to the sere & yellow leaf, there is yet that in nature which is gratifying to the eye and fills the heart with love and thankfulness to the giver of every good. The silken tassels of the corn are brown & show the ripening of the long fat cobs which ere long will fill the graneries to overflowing. Apple & peach trees are laden with their round rosy-cheeked progeny & the potatoe is equally burdened but it hides its brood in obscurity until forcibly made to give them up to light & usefulness. Then wont Paddy sure feel his mouth water at the maly mouthed crathurs. I notice a fine field of corn & pointed it out to a Frenchman sitting next to me, and asked him if he liked green corn "No" he said "we no eat corn in France. Goose eat corn, horse eat corn". I thought him a bad judge but did not say so. Nothing of importance has happened to us of late. We go on the even tenour of our way, happy in each other's love. We are very comfortable in our home, & excepting the anxieties of business, our lives pass on undisturbed by the storms & clouds of the world. I realise in my dear wife all I have hoped for or dreamed about. God be praised. We have a little project under consideration of commencing housekeeping. We have not yet determined upon it, but are much inclined to try. *Coming events* render it desirable & if on examination I find it practicable, I shall decide at once. You may therefore expect to hear more about it next mail. We have made a few friends in Newark & hope by & bye to make a nice little circle. As I have taken a year's ticket for the railroad & rents are much lower there than in the neighbourhood of New York I shall most likely settle there at least for some time to come. We have an offer of a nice little house at $125 per an. very low indeed for this country. Such an one in Brooklyn would be $300. The RRC costs $50 a year making it only $175. Then we shall be so snug & independent & have everything in real English style.

I hope you are all well and that dear Father has more employment.

Accept my dear Father & Mother the affectionate regards of

dear M.H. and Your loving son

John.

No 31 (No 30 is missing)

212 Pearl St.

JSW

New York

Jany 10th 1856

My very dear Parents,

It seems a long time since I last addressed you and that very briefly. If it had not been for the rigid observance of a plan of correspondence I should have addressed you on the late auspicious event which has from a new source renewed the reverend title of grandparents.[*] The extra cares & attention due to my dear wife in her sickness though placed last are not the least urgent pleas for my apparent neglect.

I have never had Cutler & Addy's patterns in my possession yet & intend to put the forwarding agent through whose carelessness they were seized by the Customs in Hamilton C.W. into a lawyer's hands. On this account I have not been able to do anything for Mr Bingham, & now under

[*] Their first child, Evelyn Mary, was born on 15.12.1855

the new firm I am not at liberty to do so.

Tell dear Father his congratulations are not well based. I was not so foolish as to have a boy first. My little girl will be of great use in helping to nurse the baker's dozen to follow her. She will knit & sew & make porritch when a boy would only be playing marbles or getting into mischief. And she is such a girl. I confess I did *not* believe in pretty babies until she came. But how can I withstand such conclusive evidence. Perhaps considerable credit is due to the climate of this great country. Talking of that reminds me to acquaint you with the severe weather we are now having. Last Saturday night a snowstorm came on accompanied by a strong wind, which has blocked for a while every road in the country. On looking out of doors I was almost aghast to find our house blocked up. After considerable labour I dug myself out of the drift & waded to church, in some places up to the middle of the thigh in snow. It was dry with frost & so did me no harm. This week, especially yesterday, the cold has been intense, reaching with us 6° below zero, & in some places west it is recorded as low as 20 below zero. Yesterday morning though the stove was burning till far in the morning, in our parlour the thermometer showed 14° below freezing point.

When I furnished the house I provided a Franklin stove for that room as its open grate was more cheerful & homelike but I soon found that the heat given out was not enough. Now I have a cylinder stove which is warm & comfortable. Fireplaces are of very little use in this climate so that houses are often built, as ours is, without them. The weather has been very much against MH's recovery. The cold has got into her breasts and one of them is, I fear, about to gather. She is using camphorated oil according to Dr Crane's recommendation & we are anxiously looking for the effect. In other respects she is quite well & but for this drawback & the cold weather might be out as usual. The Passaic & Hackensack rivers are frozen over, the East & Hudson Rivers are full of ice, the streets in New York are many of them impassable for vehicles, & others so blocked up that you can scarcely see across. Railroad trains often require two or three locomotives to get them along and even then are sometimes stuck. Sleighs are running in thousands of all sizes & constructions. The drivers and conductors of stage sleighs notwithstanding frequent doses of warm within & manifold wrappings of warm without are getting frostbitten. One poor fellow in

Brooklyn was all but frozen while driving. The snow is so frosted that it does not pad down at all. A sudden thaw would fill every cellar in the city and almost wash it away.

First of January this year was, as usual, a day of feasting & visiting. Mr & Mrs Crookes & I made our calls together. Our friends in Newark alone occupied us till 7.0 pm & then we proceeded to Brooklyn. Though the last train to Elizabeth was 11.45 pm we did not reach it in time & had to sleep at the American Hotel in Jersey City. I was compelled from want of time to omit many calls.

This morning there is a pleasant change in the temperature. The sun is warm as in May & the snow is softening. We have had the thermometer in Elizabeth 10° below zero. In Hartford C^y it has been 21° below zero. There is a report in this morning's paper of a stage driver having tumbled off his seat yesterday, frozen to death. Both yesterday morning & the morning before on walking up to the railroad depot at Elizt^h only about three or four minutes walk, the cold not only brought tears to my eyes but froze them on my eyelashes. It is a healthy time for all that & appetites are *very* good. The boats yesterday between New York & Brooklyn instead of being five minutes were two hours crossing the river on account of the ice. I hope the change will be good for dear M.H. & that her breast will not gather. Baby is getting very fat and only cries when hungry which is pretty often. She is always stretching & grows surprisingly. She is well supplied at the maternal fount. Hush don't tell everybody, Mary gets along very well & is very willing, is very fond of baby & would do anything for any one of us, altogether is a treasure not often met with in this country.

Adieu. My dear Parents, believe me to be as ever

Your fondly attached son John.

MHW to Mr & Mrs Webb   Chestnut St.

Elizt^h City

Feb 11th/56

My very dear Father & Mother,

As this is the first letter I have written to Sheffield since my confinement, I think it ought to be addressed to you: you have all been very

129

kind in writing to us we were very much pleased to have your kind letters last week, & return you many thanks for them. John had a letter from B & sons at the same time in which they said the money would be paid to M.A.[*] as usual so we hope you will now have no further trouble about it. You may be sure both dear John & myself are very much grieved at the discontent as expressed by the business parties in Sheffield: I cannot write to you what I think about them but of this I do know you will be firmly convinced, that no fault is due to my beloved husband: he has indeed many difficulties to contend with: I do wish Mr Pease had come out in the autumn: he would have had so much better an idea of the state of things here and the way in which orders etc. must be executed.

You will I know be pleased to hear that I went out yesterday for the first time. I have suffered much from one of my breasts having gathered & broken in two places: it is still hard on one side, but gives me no pain, so I trust it will soon be alright again. Don't you think dear John has had a good breaking in as a nurse? Indeed he has been *doctor* for I have had no other since the first three days except one visit from Dr Crane, and I am sure I have been better off without. I feel very thankful to to be quite well again; and baby is thriving famously; she is so fat & bonny: for more than a fortnight she could not draw my breast & I was obliged to use a breast pump. Therefore I had to feed her sometimes.

The snow lies on the ground still: last week we had some rain but instead of thawing the snow it was frozen on top of it so now it is completely covered with a coating of ice.

We are hoping to spend this week & next Sunday at Mr Crooke's. I have only been to Newark once since we came here. Miss Marshalls have been here several times. We have had quite a budget of letters. They came by the "Persia" the new steamer. The "Pacific" which left Liverpool 3 weeks previous to the "Persia" is not yet in port: it is supposed she is stuck in the ice, & two vessels have been sent out in search of her.

And now my dear Parents, I must conclude.

With much fond love from dear John & myself. I remain

Yours very affectionately,

Mary H Webb

[*] J.S.W. was helping to support his sister Mary Ann

Elizabeth City
March 24th 1856

My very dear Parents,

I have got an accumulation of letters to answer, for dear mother continues to be an excellent correspondent. Thank God our dreams of domestic bliss have been abundantly realised & we have received over & above a treasure which makes our heart overflow in an extasy of delight. I should be too happy if business was prosperous, that is at present the great drawback. I however live in hope & trust in God who in his own good time & way will provide. On Sunday morning Mr Mulford drove up to our front door with Mr Josh Crookes. Miss Annie Marshall & Miss Mulford & our Miss Thorp & myself joining them we proceeded to Christchurch. M.H. & Mary came on with *Evelyn Mary* when the service was partly over that the latter might not get tired & make a noise. Being Easter Sunday there was extra singing & a full church. The sun shone brightly and in thus dedicating my sweet babe to the service of God my heart felt full to overflowing. After service the whole party excepting Mr Mulford returned to our home for dinner. Evelyn was very good & seemed to think it very good fun. I was down in Philadelphia & Baltimore week before last & called on our good cousins in the former place. I should have taken M.H. down & spent Sunday there, but she had a cold & had lost her voice. She & babe are very well now. I had special cause for thankfulness in escaping a sad catastrophe which occurred only three hours after to the boat which conveys railroad passengers from Philadelphia across the Delaware to the New Jersey side. It took fire & a number of people perished in the flames & the water. . . . .

I am, as ever, Yours most affectionately,
John S. Webb

MHW Miss Susan Webb

Chestnut Str. Elizabeth N.J.
Tuesday April 29th 1856 9 pm

My very dear Sister,

We have just enjoyed a rich treat in opening the parcels so kindly sent to us from Sheffield & Manchester. . . . .

The "Persia" arrived in port at 6.30 am today, & John went over from his office about 9 o'clock to the landing place & found Mr Peace at the Customs House getting his baggage "passed". Mr P is staying in New York at present, but I suppose he will come here before long. He is a cousin of Mrs Ibbotsons, of Brooklyn, & he has other relatives here also. We (i.e. the whole family, John, baby, Mary & I) paid a visit to our friends in Brooklyn last Thursday, we stayed all night at Mr Ibbotson's and we spent Friday afternoon & Saturday morning at Mr Crookes in Newark.

John seems to like what he has seen of Mr Peace, so I hope they will get along very well together. The weather has been very warm in the last few days & everything now will be clothed with beauty. . . . .

Your fondly attached sister & friend,

Mary Hannah.

11 MHW Mr & Mrs Webb

Chestnut St. Elizabeth City N.J.

May 23rd 1856

My dear Father & Mother,

. . . .

Mr Peace is a very nice gentleman; so kind & friendly – he and dear John are on very good terms: I think each one is pleased with the other. Mr P stayed about a fortnight with us, but he is now at an hotel in New York; he preferred being somewhere near to the office, that he might go home to dinner. When he was with us he would nurse the baby all the time, he seemed so fond of her; since he left he has sent me a present of a very pretty antimacassar. I am very glad he came over and so is dear John.

Our rose trees in the front of the house are literally covered with buds which will be open next week I expect: one of them is pink and the other white, they are trained up the house. The white one has four buds together on almost every spray & on some five. Wont they look pretty? How I wish you could come and visit us in our pleasant cottage. It will be a delightful place this summer. We have a super abundance of mosquitoes already: but we must expect them, as this city is said to be "famous for pretty girls & mosquitoes". I can't say that I have seen many of the former, but I can testify to the latter abounding here. Are provisions cheap with you now? Flour has fallen about half a dollar a hundred in the last six weeks.

Evelyn grows very fast, and I can tell you she gets *very* heavy. She rolls about on the floor and looks vastly amused with everything about her.

I remain

Your very affecte daughter,

Mary Hannah Webb.

No 33

Elizabeth City

N.J.

July 31st, 1856

My very dear Parents,

. . . .

I need not hide from you that the uncertainty of my business relations has made me feel very unsettled, and I did not feel equal to epistolatory correspondence. This, thank God, is settled in such a way as to leave me somewhat better than before. I have now no direct correspondence with Sheffield except of an irregular nature, and I therefore wish you to send your letters direct to me to Elizth City N.J. and I will gladly pay the postage. It will be a good plan as we intend to write you by the first steamer every month for you to answer by the third from Liverpool, that is the third Saturday in the month. If the letters are posted in time on friday that will be soon enough. One of the Nottingham men on board the "Pacific" was running away from his creditors and taking their money. Don't you think he would sink deeper for that?

You mention George and Sarah's sixteenth wedding day. We had ours too, on the 7th, but it was only 16 months. I have endeavoured to recover Mr Bingham's patterns but not succeeded. I dare not enter a suit at law on account of the expense if I did. I think there is no doubt of a success. I saw Gervase as well as George Holmes when last in Canada & sent you a paper of which he is Editor, "The Cobourg Star". One of the articles was written by him. I am not likely to go to Canada again as we do not purpose to do any more business there, they are so long-winded.

We did not venture upstairs to bed in the winter but had a room below (now used for a nursery) fitted up, and the fire from the stove in the dining room heated it sufficiently. As regards warmth I do not think there is much difference between a well built frame & a brick house.

If we stay in Eliz^th another year we may have a nice circle of acquaintance, but that is doubtful. I wish to be nearer New York, either in Newark or Brooklyn & shall look out for that object. We often drink cold water and esteem it justly a great luxury. The heat here is too great to allow even a temporary check of perspiration so that there is no danger from its use. We do not use ice at home. Our well water is quite cold in the must sultry weather & of excellent quality. We have never had any intoxicating liquors in the house except some white brandy to put in our preserves, neither do we intend to keep any.

Mr Peace was exceedingly kind to me. I had requested him to bring me a set of table cutlery & a travelling rug, he did so, the former of ivory, 52 pieces, and did not charge me anything. I dined at his expense in the city most of the time. He gave me a pocket knife & my wife some beautiful antimacassars and other kindnesses. The cutlery was most valuable as it costs about 55% advance importing besides the heavy profits laid on in retailing.

My garden has been a source of much pleasure. I shall have quite a crop of grapes & my Indian corn is about 8 ft high. We have grown some beets & I never knew how good that sweet root is, before. Some peas which father Krauss sent are doing pretty well, but have suffered with the drought. I have some tremendous sunflowers. M.H. says they are the same kind of plant as Jack's beanstalk. We spend very pleasant evenings walking, reading, talking, nursing, gardening, etc. & are, thank God, well and happy. And now before I conclude, dear Father, let me wish you a very happy birthday, & that you may be spared to dear mother yet a many such. That God may bless you both temporally and spiritually is the fervent prayer of your affectionate son

John S. Webb

Chestnut St, Elizabeth N.J.

Aug. 21st. 1856

My very dear Father & Mother,

. . . .

You will be surprised to hear that dear John has been obliged to go to Baltimore. Messrs. Norris wrote to ask him if he could not shut up his house and take me along with him, as they might want him there two months: but we find it so much less expensive to live in our own house than to board, that we thought it best to stay, besides I should not like to part with Mary. She is such a good faithful girl and very careful. She always considers our interest & is very little expense; and we could not afford to take her with us. I was surprised and amused the other day at a doctor's fee she had to pay. She has not been in good health lately so I sent her up to our doctor's (considered the first in the city) and after stating her case he gave her a box of pills; she asked how he charged & he said 1/- but when she gave him a quarter of a dollar he gave her back 18 cents in change so that he only kept 7 cents 3½d sterling. Was not that a large fee? I am told that in Brooklyn the doctors have no smaller fee than $2 and in certain cases they charge $20 or $25. I am very glad we are not going to Brooklyn for many reasons. I have become attached to this dear little cottage – it is so snug. We have decided to stay here another year. We have had some cool weather of late. The day before yesterday was wet & stormy & I arrayed myself in a dark winter dress and fancied myself cold, & what was my astonishment on looking at the thermometer to find it stood at 70° in the shade, but that is cool after 98° as we have had it sometimes, and frequently 86°. We have very few mosquitoes here, not half so many as they have in Newark altho' our city is said to be famous for them. Our garden is very productive for its size – we scarcely buy any vegetables but potatoes. Apples are very dear this season, I am afraid they are scarce, & peaches have entirely failed.

Evelyn has only cut one tooth yet – she has another almost through. She is very fond of standing and gets up by herself when she meets with anything firm to hold by. She creeps a great deal.

I wish some of you could come and visit me in dear John's absence – it would be so nice. I do feel very lonely for we have not any friends here: our neighbours are very kind & friendly. There are some very nice walks around here, but I do not like walking alone. Mr Littlewood came here about a fortnight ago & stayed all night. He seems very fond of John & likes to visit us & always comes to the conclusion that he wants a wife himself. I wish he would marry. I am afraid he will soon be a confirmed "old bachelor".

I must now conclude as baby wants me & I have to send this to the post.

With much love to you all, I remain,

Your very affecte daughter,

Mary H. Webb

No 34   Elizabeth City N.J.

JSW   Sept 25th '56

My very dear Parents,

You will be glad to see that I am still at home. I expected to return to Baltimore after a week's visit but business in New York requires me to return some time longer. I am not at all sorry, you may be sure for I love home and thank God my home is indeed a happy one. We are pleased with the encomiums passed upon Evelyn's portrait by all our dear relatives in England & rejoice that the original is deserving of them all. She is a sweet darling & is wound round our hearts as much by her winning ways & sweet disposition as by her lovely face & the novel thrilling tie of the firstborn.

We have been papering two of our rooms, the dining room and nursery and our house looks very snug & cosy. M.H. & I bought the paper at 25 cents a piece & bordering at 5 cents a yard & put it up together. Oh that you were here to see us. Having taken the house another year we feel more settled. The landlord wanted to raise my rent $10, but I agreed to lay it out on the house so the papering is at his expense.

An instance of the uncertainty of life occurred yesterday. The gentleman who has an office next to mine died. He was at business last week, has been ailing sometime but I had no idea he was so near his end. An Englishman in the prime of life, away from all his relatives, how sad, is it not to die amongst strangers. Sawyer arrived two weeks since but I have not yet seen him. He is come out as agent for Corsan, Denton & Burdekin. I had a letter from Mr Peace this morning.

Goodnight. God bless you.

I am, as ever your affec. & dutiful son,

John S. Webb

Another brief extract from the 1897 letters will be helpful here.

Feb 22nd 1897

My dear Ethel,

. . . .

Soon after we left England Mr Brown gave up his American business to Jon^{n}. Beet & Sons of Agenoria Works, and devoted his attention to Railway Springs, the manufacture of which laid the foundation of his subsequent fortune. He made me an offer to assist him in his new works but I refused, preferring to go on with my agency for Beet & Sons. This was an unfortunate choice but I could not foresee the course which Beet & Sons took at the end of the first year. Mr Brown gave up to Jon^{n}. Beet & Sons on July 6th '55. On June 28th/56 as I could not take the responsibility of bad debts and guarantee payments for all goods I sold, they arranged with a Baltimore firm, Messrs. Norris Bros. to take the Agency. I had a legal claim on Mr Brown as our agreement was for five years but I had no desire to enforce it and as Norris Bros appeared desirous to secure my services I acted for them as New York agent, and sometimes also in Baltimore; altogether five months. I finished with them on Nov. 24/56. They offered me to take their west journey at 60 dollars a month; or would find money for me to set up an ironmongers shop in Lexington, but I refused with thanks. I now found myself in a most serious position, in a far country, with wife and child and no provision for them, the good providence of God, then as always, cared for me and mine and opened out a way for us.

J.S.W.   New York

Nov 17th/56

Dear Father,

As Mr Savage is coming to Sheffield by Wednesday steamer I send a few lines by him, knowing how anxious you will be to learn of my future course & prospects. Tomorrow is the last day of my engagement unless some new arrangement be made & up to the present moment no communications have been recd in reference to any. I expect to see Messrs. Norris or one of them soon in N.Y. but do not anticipate much result. From my letter to Lizzie you have already been made acquainted with some of my plans & projects. Employment is difficult to obtain in this city & I shall not tempt Providence by stopping to seek it. Mr S has seen M.H. & my little daughter & will tell you of the pleasant evening we passed at Mr Crookes together. M.H. has given Mary notice to leave. We can obtain a good situation for her but it will be a real grief to part with her, she is so much attached to us & fond of baby. Next Thursday will be our public thanksgiving day & in the evening Bishop Doane will hold a confirmation at St Johns. The weather is fine & pleasant though we have already had some frost to remind us of the coming winter. I cannot now answer the very kind & welcome letters from you & mother & perhaps we may not write till January. We expect to be in a throng of preparation. If we go to Dundee we shall send the most of our best furniture, being advised that the expense of freight will be less than the loss of selling & buying at the high rate of such things out there. It is no joke of a journey just a thousand miles (that is all) Please not to mention anything relating to me, out of the family.

(The letter comes to the bottom of the page at that point but it is obvious that the second half of this letter has been torn off, as there are traces of letters on the scrap of torn page.)

No 35   212 Pearl St

JSW   New York

Decr. 2nd 1856

My very dear Parents,

I take the opportunity of sending by Mr Geoe Norris who intends to sail to England by the Niagara tomorrow. I closed my business connection with him on the 24th ult. and we have been extremely busy during the past week at home packing up our furniture to go west. We proposed going on wednesday but could not get ready in time so we deferred our long journey until monday. Mr Geo Norris has been very kind & urged me to take the western journey of 2 months for them at the rate of $800 per ann. promising either to find me a permanent situation on my return or to set me up in a hardware store in Lexington V^{a}, finding me credit to any extent required. But my dear wife is very unwilling to live in a Slave state and indeed it would be very unpleasant to be deprived of liberty of speech. And for my own part I prefer the western scheme and am sanguine of success. As our furniture is almost all packed and our home uninhabitable we are at present dependant on the hospitality of our friends. We spent last weekend at our next neighbour's McCord's and took supper on sunday evening at a near neighbour's Trowbridge's. We all came over to Brooklyn yesterday morning and are now stopping at Mr Ibbotsons. We shall probably finish the week in Newark. We bade farewell to our dear pastor and his wife last week, who seemed to part with us with singular regret. He (Mr Clark) gave me a certificate in which he strongly recommended us to the care of our future pastor.

Our journey will be a costly affair. The railroad tickets through to Chicago are 22 dollars each, and the furniture may be equal to our united passage. We may possibly rest a day at Niagara Falls as the route I have chosen passes through, or rather over, the Niagara River and through Canada West. I am afraid you may blame me for taking the risk and not choosing the certainty but Mr Norris has promised to provide me a situation whenever I wish one and God has raised us up so many kind friends that it is faithless ingratitude to mistrust the future. We go direct to Carpenterville and take up a temporary abode with Mr Geo^{e} Marshall who has most kindly pressed us to do so. That village is a mile from Dundee. A brick house has just been finished in the latter place which we shall most likely rent at $100 per an. It will be best for you not to write again until we send our address, except something important should occur in which case address to Elizabeth City as heretofore. Tell Susan I was astonished to see Emma Barnett's husband standing at the door of the store in Pearl Street, No 214, next to this building. He has got a travellers situation with my neighbour's. He has been in this country three months. I brought M.H. to the office yesterday and while we were there who should

DUNDEE ACADEMY.

Mr. & Mrs. Webb, would respectfully inform the inhabitants of Dundee, and the vicinity, that they intend opening a School for the youth of both sexes, on Monday January 5th, 1857. Each term will consist of eleven weeks. Every attention will be paid to the comfort and advancement of the pupils committed to their care, or of those who wish to avail themselves of this opportunity of improvement. Hours of attendance, from 9 to 12, and from 1 to 4. The course of instruction will be as follows:

Primary Department, $5 Per Term.

| Reading, Needlework, | Spelling, Geography, | Elementary Arithmetic, Bible History, | Penmanship, Grammar, | U. S. History, Philosophy, |

Junior Department, $7.50 Per Term.

| El. Algebra, Geography, Grammar, Oratory, | Sander's H. S. Reader, Mangnall's Questions, Spelling and Defining, Greenleafs Arithmetic | Colburn's Arithmetic, History of England, Sander's Y.L. Reader Swift's Philosophy, | Book-keeping, Brewers Guide Ancient His'ry Universal " | Composition, Astronomy, El. Latin, Penmanship. |

Senior Department, $10 Per Term.

| Universal History, Astronomy, | Book-keeping, Composition, | Geometry, French, | Algebra, Oratory, | Drawing, Latin. |

Separate Day Classes.

French,bi-weekly,$5 per term | Drawing,weekly,$3 per term | Book-keeping,weekly,$3 pr.term

Evening Classes.

Penmanship, Monday, 7. p.m. | Drawing, Monday, 7 p. m. | Book-keeping Wednesday, 7 p.m.
| Arithmetic, Friday, 7 p.m. |

The departments will be sub-divided into classes, according to the ability of the pupils, and a judicious selection made for each class from the studies of the department.

visit us but Mr Littlewood and Mr Sawyer, my old chums, who were thunderstruck with the new chapter of Exodus. My not having to travel is a great inducement to my choice of life.

I am glad to hear that father has plenty of books to read; he is in clover now.

I am your very affec. son

John S. Webb

No 32   Carpenterville

JSW   Nr Dundee Ill.

December 23rd 1856

Dear Susan,

I told you in my last that I might possibly be in a novel position and sure enough I *am*. What you will all think of my scheme I cannot tell. I myself had some doubts about it, but something seemed to impel me to it, perhaps it might be my own roving inclination, perhaps the promptings of Providence. Time alone can decide. I was very much cast down on arriving here, on being told that a young lady had commenced a select school, for the place is too small for two. The prospect was dreary and I wished myself back in N.Y. I was encouraged by being advised to look about the neighbouring townships, but in such severe weather as this is (the thermometer sometimes 12° to 14° below zero) such a labour would have been discouraging besides its exhausting effect on my scanty purse. Fortunately the lady only got five pupils and gave it up in despair. I have trudged about in the deep snow with my breath frozen on my whiskers and at one house had to take off my boots to chafe my almost frozen feet, making my intentions known, and have met with tolerable success. I propose commencing school first Monday in January and shall have about 24 pupils mostly young ladies. The terms are $5 primary class & $7.50 juniors & $10 seniors.

I have taken a neat frame house at $80 per an and living here is cheap: wood $4 a cord, meat 4 or 5 c lb., flour $5 a barrel, butter 23c. considered a high price, rabbits 5c. each, potatoes 80c. a bushel, turkeys 10c. a lb. &c &c. In summer I hope to have a large school, at present many are established in other schools at a distance. So thank God we shall not starve yet. Against this we have large expenses in commencing as travelling expenses, desks, seats, another stove which alone will cost $20 & furniture in lieu of that sold by auction in Elizabeth, & above all the carriage of our furniture &c from Eliz^th which I do not think will be less than $60. We shall have hard work to make ends meet for sometime, but our prospects are improving and I have no fears for the future. The labour will be less fatiguing from the fact that all the younger children attend the District Schools, the sustaining of which is provided for by regular taxation. All pay alike whether they have children attending or not. Our school therefore will be really select as none will send children that are not pretty well advanced. We shall have a home for any of you & be glad to have you here too. I am sorry that we have no Epis^l Church here. I attended last Sunday morning the Congregational Church in Dundee and was pleased with the singing and sermon. Besides this are the Baptist, Methodist & Scottish Ch. The spiritualists or spirit rappers have what they call a church, a singular looking round building with tinned dome about a mile from here, near the top of the hill backed by woods. Here the mediums have their trances and profess to bring news from the spirit world. My own landlord, Mr Austin, is a firm believer in this humbug.

Our friends have not failed us in our necessity. Since the first of this month we have enjoyed their society and hospitality. Mr Marshall whose kindness is the more remarkable from our being comparatively strangers gave us a warm welcome here, & we are staying at his house until our own is ready. It was through his representations in answer to a letter of mine that induced me to come West.

Last summer there were numerous cases of cholera and yellow fever in N.Y. At present scarlet fever is prevalent in some parts of the East especially Newark N.J. I do not wish to return to England except on a visit.

I am your affec. brother, John S. Webb

MHW Mr & Mrs Webb

Dundee, Kane Co. Ill.

March 18/57

My dear Father & Mother,

The welcome budget from Sheffield and Aughton gave us much pleasure. It is very kind of you to write us such nice long letters; it is quite a treat to receive them. We seem to be almost out of the world here, we seldom or never see a newspaper except our little Tribune from Elizabeth town which has been forwarded to us to complete our year's subscription. I wish you would send us a paper now & then when you think the news will interest us. I am not going to answer your kind letters now, but just to fulfill one request of yours, dear Mother, viz: that I would give you an account of my way of cooking &c. I suppose you are aware that the cook stoves have ovens attached. The one we have now is almost square. There are four round lids on the top which lift up and in any of which we can place our kettle or saucepans – the fire is at the front of the stove, and the oven behind and underneath it. The heat is conveyed all round, so that it is just as hot at the bottom as at the top. To heat the oven I have only to put some pieces of dry wood on the fire, shut up the front doors of the stove and draw out the damper and it is ready in a few minutes. I have not had much practice in the art of confectionery for we have always lived very plainly. Our principal food is bread: I make a sweet cake now and then. I have only made three since we came here. We live chiefly on brown bread which we both prefer to white. I make it by saving a piece of leaven from each baking, set it in sponge for about an hour, then knead it with a little salaratus (which is a kind of soda) & a *great deal* of water, and pour it into tins, let it rise for about 2 hours then bake it nearly an hour. I make white bread in the same way only kneading it stiffer. There is no baker's shop here & yeast is not to be had at any price. We usually have what we call pancakes in a morning, they are an imitation of buckwheat. They are made of unbolted flour mixed to a thick batter with some saved from each day to raise them – also a little salaratus. I mix them after tea every evening & add a little warm water & the salaratus. In the morning then fry them with a little lard, two at a time on a griddle which is a kind of long frying pan with a handle at each end & which fits into the stove: we eat them with butter or treacle.

We have almost learned to live without meat for it is seldom we can get it here. One of the pupils brought us a rabbit about three weeks ago & it lasted us three days. We were two whole weeks without tasting meat, but now have got a nice large leg of pork which will last a long time: we neither of us care for meat now, though; once we thought we could not live without it. We get a quart of good milk every day and baby thrives on it wonderfully. She has some thickened with flour in a morning also at night

143

just before we go to bed, a little pudding made in a saucer for dinner & a cup of milk for tea: I forget, I did not tell you she has weaned. Mr Marshall came down here a day or two after I last wrote to Susan, & offered to take her up to their house & as I was suffering very much at the time from my gathered breast, I was glad to let her go. Mrs M. kept her four days & they said she was no trouble at all after the first night. Mr M. said that "a better child never entered anyone's house", he is so fond of her. My breast broke again while she was away and then it began to heal. It is now quite well & I am enjoying good health. I have been out several times. We have made several calls in the village. I think we shall find some pleasant society before long.

From the accounts we receive from our friends in Brooklyn, Newark, &c it seems they have as severe a winter as we have. Mrs Ibbotson who has lived in Brooklyn 21 years says she never experienced anything like it before. I am rejoiced to think it is now over: we shall soon have spring and then the country will be beautiful. It is just two years since *our* visit to Spring Lane! I wonder when we shall see all our beloved friends again I assure you I did all in my power to persuade dear John to go to England instead of coming here, but I found that he would not be happy to do it then, so I determined still to "Hope on" someday I trust we shall all meet again "Oh that will be joyful!" Dear John will never be content to be under Mr Brown again. I am sure he has not behaved kindly to him. What do you think he has done? Why written to parties here for a statement of their account with requests for immediate payment to Sheffield, when John had sent him a statement of the accounts being paid as long ago as July last. The money was paid to Mr Peace for the new firm by order of the solicitors – now the parties are seeking John in New York or writing to him for an explanation & of course his character is impugned by it. Is it not unpleasant? He has really not had time to write to Mr B & look after his affairs since we came here & I am sure it is too bad.

Dear John says the mails in winter are generally a week from New York or Boston and in summer about three days. We have nothing more to pay on them.

I must now conclude hoping you are all well,

Believe me ever your own loving and affectionate daughter,

Mary Hannah Webb

No 36   Dundee Kane Coy Ill.

JSW   April 7 1857

Mr & Mrs Webb,

My dear Parents,

Before I write about anything else I must express my hearty thanks
for no less than five letters which I have received since I last addressed
you, the last of which came in company with no less than *eighteen* letters.
I will now answer all your queries as far as I am able. I should not like to
be with Mr B. after being my own master and breathing the atmosphere of
freedom. It would be like going to work in the plantations in Louisiana. I
am not afraid of making a livelihood here, for if one way will not lead to
it another will. My present scheme has not succeeded as well as I hoped it
would & I know not yet whether I shall have to strike my tent & seek a
better pasture.

We also enjoy the inestimable blessing of good health, and do not
find the hardship to be very hard, for we have many comforts to soften
them down. As for our cares & anxieties we cast them all upon the Lord and
hitherto he has fulfilled his promise. We have many kind friends and
have experienced much cordiality, even from strangers. Most of the winter
the severe weather and dear M.H.'s sickness prevented our visiting, but
latterly we have made quite a number of visits together.

I endeavoured to see Mr Child at Suspension Bridge when passing
through on my way hither, but could not meet with him. I have since
written to him about the patterns & had no reply. As regard Mr Brown's
agreement I am too proud and independant to want any man's money unless
I render the worth of it and have released him from all obligations. We
laughed at your idea of a Brewery or Restaurant, of the former I have had
enough & the latter is quite out of my line. I hope your insurance agencies
will be profitable. Have you done anything in it yet?

I do not think it possible in the present way of doing business in this
country to obtain the kind of commissions father speaks of. Every
Sheffield house of any note has its agent to deal with the parties on the
spot, & many of the merchants come over to England to transact their own
business. If I can I will send you one of our circulars. Our terms are $3.50,
5.00, 7.50 & $10 according to the age or studies pursued which are equal in

145

English money to 14/-, 20/5, 28/7, 30/8, 40/10 we have none of the last as yet. I regret to say that nearly half of our pupils the present quarter are under 10 years at 14/- & the rest at 20/5. Fortunately living is cheap & we have a better prospect for another term if we determine to remain. I have written to Mr Brown about business affairs but do not choose to make him a confidante in my private matters. Because I tell you, there is no reason that tout le monde should know.

Dundee has a population of 1600 but looks small as the nucleus is small & many are scattered about. Fifteen of my pupils last term came under the junior department of 30/8 & I had a very interesting school. This term there is more plodding work & more real labour, with less remuneration. You may know what our income is when I tell you that I number only thirteen. We look for more though before the term is through.

Christmas is not much kept here as New Year is more popular. We had a roast turkey at Mr Marshall's on the occasion. I shall have a famous garden. It is not yet fenced in, but will measure 151 ft. by 60 & contains 8190 sq ft after deducting the area of the house. We brought some seeds from Elizabeth City and I have bought some more here. I have sown some tomatoes in a box to be ready to plant out early and was busy last friday after school and all day on saturday laying out walks and putting on gravel. The latter was on the spot, having been dug out of the cellar and basement of the house. The soil is apparently a rich black loam with a substratum of gravel. Part of the garden is on a steep decline and I am afraid that the gravel crops out on it but cannot tell till I dig it up.

I have had no Sheffield paper in a long time. Mr Crookes arranged to send his but on enquiry was told that it was a great expense to send one from New York. I believe he either misapprehended or was misinformed. When you have one to spare please send it but do not be at any expense in procuring one. I should like to see a copy of the Daily Telegraph. There are two hardware stores here which is one too many for this small place, consequently no room for me to do any trade.

I cannot describe the serpents of Illinois as I have neither seen nor heard of them. Oh yes, I'm forgetting, I remember turning over a worm on saturday. Of wild beasts a small kind of wolf is the worst and deer the best. I prefer the latter though if I were so fortunate as to knock one of the former over I might obtain four dollars for his head of the town authorities. Neither are numerous. Of the game we had a taste last sunday in the shape of a canvass backed duck which we relished exceedingly.

One of my pupils last

(this letter has covered one quarto sheet written both sides and both ways. The last incomplete sentence suggests that a whole page is missing)

No 37

JSW

Dundee Kane Co. Ill.

Augt 14th 1857

My dear parents

Your welcome letters of April 20th & June 1st came duly to hand & quite a number of newspapers for which I am gratefully obliged. I have not lost all interest in our old smoky town & like to know what is going on there. I am glad to hear that Sheffield is not lagging in the rear of progress. I was astonished to find that it contains sufficient enterprise to establish a daily paper. The Daily Telegraph is I think below the Independant in its moral tone & in other respects inferior. The last paper rec^d from you was the Manch^r Courier containing the visit of the Queen to the Art Exhibition. I do not take a New York paper but have the opportunity of reading the Weekly Tribune, & our Elizth City paper the Jersey Tribune is still sent to us. During term time I have very little time for reading, one duty treads on the heels of another leaving few idle moments.

We have been paying lately nearly as much for flour as the price you state. Here it is $3.25 per 100 lbs. or 1/10¼ per stone. We shall have it much cheaper as the farmers are now realising a splendid harvest. A pleasanter summer than this I never experienced. We have had hot weather but the Prairie breeze prevents sultryness. The greatest heat we have noticed was 110° in the sun, which is not much felt when the air is in motion. The atmosphere is not so dry as in the East. With the exception of the cutting North wind in winter, I am of opinion that our climate is much pleasanter than that of New York.

Our dear little Evelyn is a well-spring of joy. She enjoys very good health & is cheerful & good tempered. Our great regret is that her grandparents cannot share our parental delight. She grows slowly but is well formed. You will laugh when I tell you that since we left Eliz^th City, where we used a cradle lent to us by a neighbour, her cot has been the tray which fitted in the top of my large sea chest. The chest itself is no less useful as it stands in the pantry as a receptacle for our bags of flour, sugar, &c &c. A short time ago I bought Eva a nice little wicker carriage which at the same time is a pleasure to her & convenient to us. She was becoming too heavy to carry any distance. She talks very little but is now trying very hard. She is very fond of sugar for which she sounds "sh". She tells everyone that her 'olly broke' for dolly is broken; for cow she says moo, for dog boh &c &c. In every picture she sees containing a man or a woman she calls the one *pa* & the other *ma.* She often points to grandpa's portrait which hangs in the chamber & calls it *pa.* We put her to bed awake after dinner & towards 8 at night. She sleeps an hour or two in the afternoon. A country life suits her well she spends a long time looking at the cows & horses of which numbers run at large. She has not been the least trouble in the garden. It is sufficient to tell her not to touch this or that. She amuses herself chiefly with the gravel on the walk or the wild flowers on the grass. Excuse my enlarging on this theme.

The scenery here is just what I like. I do not speak of Dundee alone, but the country all around. Nothing majestic but teeming fertile plains, secluded fertile valleys, deep glens, sombre with overshadowing oaks, the river sparkling in sunbeams seen here & there through the trees, the road winding sometimes through woods, then along well cultivated farms with pretty homesteads & fine cattle roaming on the road. In some instances we may discern the progressive course of prosperity in the log hut, the larger plank dwelling & the aspiring brick house on the same farm. With the enjoyment of Nature's loveliness we can command as good society as in a city, instead of the Indians and snakes, bears & wolves amongst which father places us. Of all these I have seen but one specimen and that was a harmless water snake two feet long which I killed near the schoolhouse. I could go hundreds of miles further west and yet enjoy all the accustomed appliances of civilized life. As for Nova Scotia, I consider it far behind, there is more fogeyism there than in England & its natural advantages are inferior. Both MH & I thought Halifax a miserable looking place.

Our garden is now repaying the labor & expense which has been laid out on it. We had an abundant daily supply of most delicious lettuce, then followed about a doz good boilings of peas of which we might have had more but for the large quantity of seed I wished to save. There is no dependance on seed bought at the stores as it is frequently mixed or labled [sic] incorrectly. Besides my peas were mostly from some excellent kinds sent over by father Krauss. The cucumbers succeeded the peas. Mine are a small kind called the early cluster cucumber growing about 7 or 8 inches long & most convenient size for a small family. The Indian corn & Potatoes we have tried & found very good but not yet full grown. My corn is gigantic some being over ten feet high. The Beets also we are using. The Cabbage is coming on, some we have cut as greens to thin the plants a little. We also boiled some of the white beet tops & found them as good as spinach. Turnips, carrots, beets & parsnips are all ready. Pumpkins, Squashes, Melons, and Citrons are all doing well and some have large fruit on. We have quantities of tomatoes but none ripe. All the fruit we have is on one little apple tree which is tolerably full. Our friends are very kind in sending us fruit, as currants, green, red & black, & gooseberries. M.H. preserved 15 quarts of Red Currants & 6 of Black. We paid 2½d. sterling for red & 3d for black. We have already got some cucumbers & tomatoes in pickle & shall add all kinds of things from time to time. We have cultivated but few flowers, nasturtiums convolvulus & canarienses are all except some french marigolds self sown from the sweepings of the classroom. Yesterday I was busy mowing the grass so we now look quite prim.

You need not be afraid of us starving ourselves. We have generally good appetites & plenty to satisfy them. We can get meat whenever we want it as another butcher has set up business over the river. The great difficulty is to get a piece small enough to keep good till eaten. A bit of lamb 1¼ lbs which I got yesterday for ten cents served us for two dinners, costing only 1¼ d each per meal.

We are both very glad that George is not likely to leave Aughton as the most interesting event of our life is connected with that place & we hope some day to revisit scenes pregnant with pleasant recollections.

There was another fall of rock at Niagara Falls. On 2nd Augt about 100 tons fell from the precipice at Goat Island about 300 feet below the British Falls. Four persons were beneath it at the time & three of them were hurt. When I last wrote to you we were enjoying a visit from Mr James Banning from Manchester. He arrived on 6th of July and left us on the 13th. He brought us a parcel from the Krausses containing amongst a number of useful dress pieces &c, a portrait of our late brother Charles & the only one ever taken of him. Mr B enjoyed himself though we were both engaged at the time with our school duties. In the evenings we took long rambles together & on the saturday borrowed Mr Marshall's buggy & drove over to Crystal Lake, a pleasant place ten miles distant where we picniced in the woods & enjoyed ourselves in a quiet way. He has two sisters living in the western part of this State at Quincy also a brother near there. He came in at New Orleans & after leaving us intended going through Canada to New York & after visiting Boston, Philad, Baltimore & Washington to return to England. A very nice trip, was it not? We took a pretty long one the other night, visiting Salt Lake Vally & California. I mean we went to see a panorama of the overland route which proved with the descriptions of the exhibitor very interesting. Though the half of our holidays are over we have scarcely begun to enjoy them. Most of the first week was occupied in house cleaning in which I took quite a conspicuous position. If you had seen me taking up & shaking carpets, sweeping, scouring floors, white-washing ceilings, color washing walls &c &c I think you would have hired me for housemaid right off. We both look and feel clean & comfortable. I could not get any good white lime but what was air slaked & that rubs off easily so I was forced to be content with water lime which is a bad color. We mixed a little blue into the ceiling wash & vermilion into the wall wash, tinting it a delicate salmon colour which formed a nice contrast with the white. I hung up two of the large engravings which we had in Elizth in the parlor having replaced the smashed glasses in Elgin & they make the room quite spicy. The house cleaning over I had some bookkeeping for Mr Marshall & M.H. had heaps of sewing & darning. Last saturday Mr Marshall & I went over to Crystal Lake to make some enquiry about an academy there which is at present closed. It was built by a company of shareholders, the ground (five acres) being given. The building cost $2700. Owing to disagreement amongst the directors & mismanagement the school has not prospered & they want immediate means raising, to pay

150

off a debt of one thousand dollars. For this purpose they offer the building for $1800 dollars [sic] land included. Though a great bargain I cannot do this for want of the needful. It is an excellent location being a place of resort in summertime from Chicago. A strong objection is the building is entirely for school purposes one above & one on ground floor with 2 classrooms to each, with no convenience for a dwelling house and no cellar. We have done pretty well so far, having paid our expenses and got a little money in hand. We have much to be thankful for and in numerous instances of God's good providence. What the future will bring forth we cannot tell but have no reason to be anxious. Our expenses have been small and our wants few. Whether we remain in Dundee depends on our success during the winter. No man needs to want in this country. With resolution & diligence even a fortune may be gained, & I look forward to the time when I shall sit under my own vine & see smiling acres around to call my own. I might have kept a cow all the summer with no cost except her price as there is plenty of free pasture & have kept her all the winter for $10. We are so short of time that we could not look after her. Perhaps when I can buy a little land I shall farm in summer & keep school in winter as so few attend during the summer months.

We had an invitation yesterday to a supper which Mr Marshall was giving his workmen in the evening. We had supper in the Factory and after full justice had been done to the plentiful viands were entertained with speeches sentiments songs & dancing to violin & flute & then went to bed at 2 am at Mr Marshall's. Mr M. is a manufacturer of reaping & mowing machines & the treat was on occasion of the end of the season for making them. We arrived home after breakfast towards 9 AM. I should tell you there were no less than six babies there & all very good. Eva slept soundly laid in her little carriage. As soon as I got home I measured our house that I might send you the view & plan according to your wish. The view is merely from memory as I had not time to take a regular sketch. The ground in front has not yet been levelled off. The plan is to scale about 1/27 in to the foot, but the figures attached to it will tell you at once the size of each room. I have marked the stove pipe in the school room though the stove is now put by for the summer, that you may judge of the trouble I had in taking it down so frequently. The stove is so close as to warm both rooms which it does effectually.

151

The church is a plain brick edifice with a square wooden belfry tower painted white. We have a good preacher. We have visited little yet. We supped at Mr Young's, the baptist minister, last week & propose to take a little trip by rail this week to Aurora & Elgin & on our return canvas Dundee for scholars. I do not know whether the school will pay us in the future as it has done & we have my remuneration for the District School in hand to make up any deficiency. If Dundee cannot keep us I shall look out for a better place in the spring, I think. I never was happier in my life than during this summer, & have I not abundant cause.

We never have our doors all fastened at night, & have even slept with one open wide. No need for fire arms except for game.

With much love Your Affect son John.

P.S. I have got some tansy in the garden of which M.H. has flavoured several puddings. We like it much, would not father like to have some of it from us?

Prices in Dundee. Black tea 2/6 Green 3/- West Indies 9d Sugar 6½d – 9d lb. Beef, mutton veal 4d Pork 7 salted in pickle.

Mr & Mrs Webb
MHW

Dundee Kane Co. Ill.
Oct 2nd 1857

My very dear Parents,

We enjoyed our little pleasure trip very much & I think the change of scene did us all good. We went first to Geneva by railroad, that is a pretty little place on the Fox River, it is our county town. We walked about a little to inspect it, but found nothing very remarkable excepting some splendid *double* sunflowers which were growing in a garden; as we were looking at them we saw a lady & gent (the owners of the garden) & they entered into conversation with us & invited us to go into their garden which we did & admired it much. We dined at the Hotel & after dinner set out to walk to Batavia, another town on the Fox River which we wished to visit. The distance by road is only three miles, by railroad it is ten, & the train would not have taken us there before evening so after walking

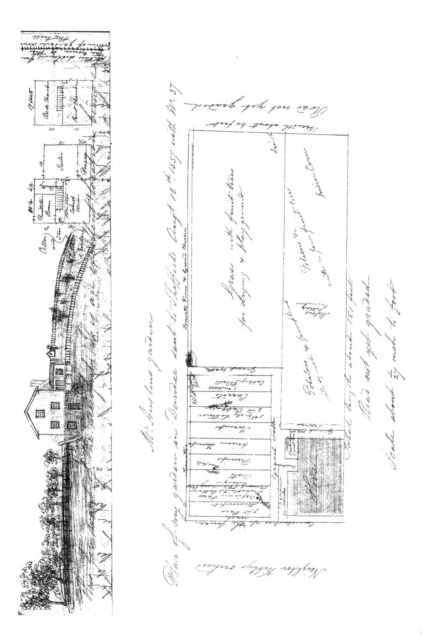

Plan of J.S.W.'s garden in Dundee

153

about half way we were overtaken by a wagon going to the stone quarry at Batavia (which is very extensive & valuable) & we rode the remainder of the distance; we walked about for two or three hours & about 7 PM started by train for Aurora. We arrived there before eight o'clock, called at Mr Rippon's store & he went with us to his house which is a very nice one. Both he & his wife received us very kindly and treated us with the greatest hospitality altho' we were almost entire strangers to them. We intended leaving the next day, Friday, but nothing would satisfy them but our staying till Monday so we did not leave until 6.30 AM on Monday. The distance from here is only 28 miles, & yet we could not get home before 1.30 PM. We had to wait about $4\frac{1}{2}$ hours at a junction on the railway. After our return home we took several long walks canvassing for pupils but without any present success. We have not a large school yet, but John seems very sanguine about next term. I help him each afternoon; & I have two pupils for French; but I am not quite so busy as before the holidays having the mornings for my own work.

. . . .

We do not often go to Church together: as Eva is too great a fidget to take with us, but last Sunday we left her with our neighbours & both went, & John went alone in the afternoon to hear a coloured minister preach. Mr Hibbard gave out the strangest notice I ever heard given in any church. It was that we were *all* requested to be present at the "House" (so they always style the church) next Saturday morning as early as eight o'clock & to bring with us as many other persons as we could induce to come for the purpose of renovating it, as, he said, it had become altogether too dirty for divine worship!! It is a very nice neat little church tho' it has no architectural pretensions. I wish we had an Episcopal church here.

Aurora is a very pretty as well as a thriving place: it is the largest town on the Fox River, contains about 6000 inhabitants. Property which four years ago sold for 400 dollars now demand 1800. There are several churches & a large Institute is building which is intended to accommodate 300 boarders. I should like to live there better than in any other place I have seen, but of course there is no opening for a private school. We met with several English people there, and some very agreeable ones too. Mr Rippon's Father & Mother live next door to them; they have been many years in this country yet they still speak broad Sheffield dialect. They have three sons & a daughter in California. We are beginning to feel that winter will soon be here: two nights ago we had a sharp frost which killed our tomato plants, also the melons, squashes, pumpkins etc. We have had the stove up in our sitting room nearly a fortnight & find a fire very comfortable. Evelyn begins to talk a great deal in her way, tho' that is not very intelligible, the children are all so fond of her that they almost quarrel about having her at noon & recess. I suppose you have seen account of the loss of "Central America". Was it not an awful wreck?

We have had a splendid harvest this season & I suppose flour will soon be very cheap. Potatoes are now selling from 10 to 15 cents per bushel (60 lbs), is not that very low. John says they are not worth growing, for he paid a dollar a bushel for the seed and ours have not yielded very well, they have the rot among them. Sugar is now a little cheaper. We paid 14 cents per pound for some we bought last week – butter 19 cents per pound.

With much love to dear M.A., Susan & Lizzie & a large portion for yourselves.

I remain your very affect^e daughter

Mary Hannah

P.S. Best flour from winter wheat is now 1/9d per stone sterling will be cheaper soon I expect 1/5½d

No 34   Dundee Kane Co Ill.
JSW   Nov 21st 1857

My Very Dear Sister Susan,

As it is not quite six months since I last wrote you it may be a matter of surprise that I should address you again so soon. Joking apart, please accept my former excuses.

. . . .

Our Fall Term terminated on 16th last Monday and on the 18th we commenced our winter term. The attendance is small owing to the severe weather but our prospects are good. I completed some carpenter work last week which I hope will conduce greatly to our comfort during the winter. I have boarded up a portion of the piazza in front so as to enclose two outer doors, one leading into the parlour & the other into the schoolroom, nailing up the latter altogether & using the enclosed part as a closet for hats, coats & wood for parlour use. We now enter the house by a gate into the garden close by & in at the back parlour door, the scholars are using the recitation room door. To secure the parlour from the visits of Jack Frost I have made porch to the back door of planed boards same as the front jointed & driven together roof floor & door complete about 4 feet square. The door to it is one I took away from between the recitation & schoolroom. We hope now to find our home more tolerable. I only just finished in time as we have now a snowstorm on hand & a terribly cold wind. Already the railway trains on our road have been prevented running regularly by the drifts. The cold came upon us so suddenly that we almost despaired getting in our roots, but an auspicious softening gave me the opportunity of housing the remnants of our garden produce.

We have been fortunate in obtaining a help on advantageous terms. Her name is Henrietta Adeline Baxter, she is an orphan adopted by one of our best citizens. She is to board with us & attend school, Mr Oatman paying for her tuition & her services out of school to be at our disposal. She is a good girl, about 20.

Winter has commenced early. Our first severe frost was on the last night of September & a snowstorm commenced last Wednesday which is receiving additions from time to time & promises to last some while. Unfortunately our soft water system which had been out of repair all the summer was only cemented just before the frost set in and is therefore empty. The landlord promised to do it in the spring, but I was obliged to threaten him with non-payment of rent before I could persuade him to do it. I have to fetch hard water from the bottom of the hill before our house, which labor makes us thoroughly appreciate the value of water. I often laugh when I contrast my different mode of life in Sheffield, New York & Dundee. Here I literally hew my own wood, draw my own water, & carpenter, glazier, errand boy, gardener, carrier, school teacher, accountant, nurse, housemaid, student &c &c delighting all the time in my freedom from conventionality & the whims & petty tyranies of so called masters a name which in America has been long banished south [sic] of Mason & Dixon's line.

We have got a new bridge across the river over which teams first passed on the 28th Octr. I was very glad for we were wanting coal for our schoolroom stove & were obliged to burn short bits of wood in it. I had our winter stock carted from the depot & having taken some of a large lot bought by Mr Marshall I only paid $5 per ton delivered. M.H. & I had a nice drive to Elgin on the 10th Octr. The road is well wooded & looked charming in its autumnal pink. We brought back a neat cane rocking chair which Eva calls Ma's chair, also a large & small bell for the use of the school which we had long wanted. Produce is cheap here. I paid only $2 per 100 lbs for the last lot of white flour and 1d sterling per lb also $1.50 for 100 lb brown flour. 37½ c. for 25 lbs Buckwheat flour 20c. lb Butter 8c. per lb Beef 10c. Pork. Potatoes are 25c. bushel Best Eating Apples £1.00 Pie apples 50c. Our Manchester friends quote long prices for these articles. Please to tell us what you pay in the next. My potatoes were not prolific but we raised between 7 & 8 bushels. These with the turnips, carrots, beets, parsnips & squashes will last us most of the winter. We have, thank God, a more comfortable prospect than the same time last year, are very snugly settled, usefully employed & happy in each other's love. Usefulness & happiness must I believe, go hand in hand. Next Thursday is Thanksgiving Day in our State & I suppose we shall have holidays, also on Xmas & new year's day, but no vacation as in England. I daresay you are looking forward to a release from your severe duties & we hope that you will enjoy your leisure very much.

       With love to each and all dear Susan,
              Your loving brother John

Another extract from the 1897 letters may be of interest here:

Dear Ethel,

       I don't intend to write much tonight but would like to add a few more lines about our life in Dundee. I have mentioned Mr Young the Baptist Minister. One day in the depth of winter I saw an extraordinary sight; a number of people were being baptised in the river. A hole had been cut in the ice, and Mr Young stood in the water, dipping them. As they came out of the water, their clothes soaked and dripping, they wrapped themselves up and in this condition were driven home in their buggies. Mrs

Young afterwards told me she never felt any anxiety about evil results to her husband. A different & pleasanter sight on the river on a summer night was fish-spearing (I think for eels). We have sat up in bed looking at the boats which carried bright lights to attract the fish. The best fish for eating were the black or rock bass, but they are not nice to take hold of, their fin spines are so sharp; I had my hand cut with a live one.

The best birds for the table were the canvas-back duck, and the prairie hen. All through the winter the river was frozen a great thickness, and holes had to be made in the ice to get in the water. The sleighs were usually driven on it instead of on the road. When summer approached, or rather as soon as winter was over, our school was very much reduced in numbers, as the youths only attend school in the winter term, and work on the farms while the season is available. But, nil desperandum as one door shuts another opens. The District School Directors and my friend Dr Goodwin in particular urged me to undertake it for the summer session and they engaged the doctor's daughter as my assistant.

We had on the whole a happy time in Dundee and the kind of life was to me very enjoyable. The climate suited me, though in winter our sitting room, with a hot stove in the middle, would have its walls sparkling with icy diamonds, and at such time we would bring down our bedding at night and lie by the side of the stove, and take care to keep it burning all night.

Besides friendly visits we had meetings for discussion on subjects previously arranged, the persons to move the affirmative and objective being also fixed. Americans delight in public speaking, so these meetings were generally very lively. They were held at the District School House (on the far side of the river where were also some houses) at "early candlelight", and each one would take his lamp or lantern and set it on the desk before his seat. All would go: lawyer, squire, shopkeeper, teacher etc. etc and try to decide such knotted points as "Whether money or women had most influence".

Very little money circulated. If A owed B, he would give him an order for the amount on C, a shopkeeper, who owed A for produce and so there was a regular system of barter. The absence of conventionalism was delightful, and also the dignity of labour was remarkable. I found Mr Young, the Baptist minster at the washtub one day, and he was not shamed at being seen. And when it was known that Mr Hibbert the Congregational Minister let his wife fetch water instead of going himself, he was blamed.

From your affectionate
John S. Webb

No 38

JSW

Dundee Kane Co. Ill.
Decr 28th 1857

My very dear Parents,

I have before me five of your kind & newsful letters, the last received on Xmas Eve only four hours before a certain interesting event, of which more anon.

I am not likely to hear of Cutler. I guess he will find Utah a hot place by & bye, as the Mormons are in an attitude of defiance towards the Federal Government & a military expedition was sent against them this year but too late to come into action.

There is a direct water communication from Chicago to England but only by small transient vessels. If we should come to England from Dundee which as yet is very doubtful (parliament not yet having voted the supplies) it would be by way of Montreal if in summer & New York, Boston or Philadelphia in winter as I would not then venture through the Gulf of St. Lawrence. The cost of the passage I have not ascertained. John Krauss Webb has not arrived so that I cannot gratify you with a grandson of that name.

We have fog here sometimes a necessary consequence of living in a river valley, but they are neither frequent nor troublesome. I am very glad that provisions are cheaper with you but still you cannot get beef at our price: 6 cents or 3d a pound. During the first half of this term we have had but a few pupils, but are expecting more after the holidays. I found it to be both policy and conveniency to give a little vacation so we broke up on thursday evening & recommence next monday the 4th. The stove pipe has done pretty well so far & I hope by good management to have less trouble with it.

I told you that we had got a help so that since the commencement of the present term six weeks ago, dear M.H. has been relieved of her heavier household duties. She continues with us, & for an American help is tolerable. She is willing & can wash, bake & iron but is very ignorant & like all other folk with few ideas, has the greatest idea of herself. Though ours is but a village we are not without resources of a literary nature. I have the privilege of borrowing books from the Library of the Division of Sons of Temperance of which I am a member & have frequently attended their Wednesday evening meeting which is sometimes very interesting. We have lately set on foot a Lyceum or Debating Club which promises to be a lively source of pleasure & profit through the winter. There have already been three regular meetings & one this evening, now in session makes a fourth. The subject for debate & the disputants are chosen at the preceding meeting. The following is a list of those which have already been presented with the side. I took on the question "The influence of women is greater than that of money" affirmative. "Education is not worth the trouble or expense of its acquisition" – neg. "The sea exhibits more wonder than the land" – aff. "Women ought to have all the rights & privileges socially, morally & politically that man has". On the last I should have taken the affirmative but circumstances prevented my attendance. Last monday in addition to my part in debate I had to give an address. The order of proceedings includes an oration or declaration or essay. With all this practice I hope soon to acquire a little skill as a public speaker. We are favored in Dundee by occasional lectures by professional lecturers. A course we had lately on Physiology illustrated by a French mannikin were very good. The sermons by Mr Hibberd are also literary treats. He is very painstaking & studies hard, he is well read & uses very good language. His preaching has also the unction of sincere & earnest piety.

Your surmises or intelligence respecting my dear wife's condition were correct, she had been uncomfortable through the week & it was chiefly on her account that I gave holiday. She chose or rather it happened at a most convenient time. On Thursday noon I call on Dr Goodwin to engage his services & at 5 PM I sent down to an experienced neighbour, Mrs Vining the lawyer's wife, who had volunteered her services. At seven I fetched the doctor & at ¼ to 9 my dear wife was safely delivered of a pretty little *girl*. She is very smart & will I trust very soon recover her strength. You would laugh to see what a funny little chamber we made or rather fitted up for the occasion. I told you in Susan's letter that I had enclosed a portion of the piazza which formed a closet out of the parlor, I had no idea what purpose it would serve when I made it but necessity forced its adoption. We could not have a stove in either of the chambers as there was no place for a stovepipe, the basement kitchen was too damp & the parlor liable to intrusion. The previous saturday (the 19th) we therefore got some wallpaper & put it on the closet, & fixed up the bedstead in it, & put a carpet down making it quite snug & prim. The door into the parlor is kept open except when occasion required & the stove there keeps up a pleasant warmth.

I like it so well that I shall occupy it all winter & be saved the trouble I had last winter if making a bed in the parlor & carrying it away every morning. Please send us some names for baby.

With much love we are your most affec^y

J.S. & M.H. Webb

P.S. a lock of Eva's & baby's hair enclosed.
Eva weighed today 24$^3/_4$ lb & baby 7$^1/_4$ lb or 7 lb 13 oz.

Dec. 29th 9$^1/_2$ AM Dear M.H. & baby are both very smart. M.H. is going to have chicken for dinner.

M & Mrs Webb

MHW

Dundee Kane Co Ill.

Feb 8th 1858

My very dear Parents,

You will learn from dear John's letter to George what an affliction we have been called to pass through, & I know you will sympathise with us most deeply. Would that we could receive your words of comfort & consolation now while our hearts are bleeding under the stroke! Thanks be to God we have not been left without comfort: our Heavenly Father has been near to us & made us feel that 'all things work together for good' & that his chastisement has been sent in love for our profit; & we earnestly pray that it may be the means of drawing us nearer to God, and making us "set our affections on things above, not on things of the earth". It was indeed a severe trial to lay our sweet darling in the cold ground – so young, so lovely, so beloved! but we feel that God has taken her to himself, & she is now far happier than we could ever make her. When laid in the coffin she looked most beautiful – some who saw her said "like a little angel". She breathed her last so gently that she seemed to be asleep. She suffered much in the first part of her illness having at times violent paroxysms of pain, almost like spasms, which lasted two hours or more & between them she would moan so piteously, it made our hearts ache to hear her: she could not draw my milk any of the time except the last Sunday, Monday & part of Tuesday when she seemed to be getting a little better; after that time she gradually became weaker, but at the same time seemed to suffer less, & slept a great deal. Dr Goodwin was very kind & attentive & did all in his power to save her, sometimes he came three times in a day, but from the first he gave us very little hope, as he said her lungs were very much diseased – she had great difficulty in breathing, & we had to apply mustard poultices to her chest & back several times in a day, also onions, bread & milk, fomentations of hops, smart weeds, & many other things to keep her skin moist & relieve her breathing. She took medecine every three hours, and stimulants or nourishment between. I had not apprehended any immediate danger the night she died & laid down to sleep, a little while, with her on my arm, where she slept very quietly & seemed more comfortable than I had seen her during most part of her illness: about half past one AM on Friday I got up & sat by the fire to give her medicine, & then fed her with a little arrowroot but it seemed only to trickle down her throat, and soon after she gasped two or three times and then threw up some dark fluid from her stomach, and then both breath & pulse ceased. Dear John immediately ran to fetch Mrs Vining who has been very kind to us ever since baby's birth, and who lives just at the bottom of our garden, & she came immediately & Mr V. also before the little darling casket had become cold, but too late to apply any remedy – they stayed until 4 o'clock and performed the last sad offices for our precious child, excepting laying her in the coffin which Mr V did on Saturday morning. We had many callers on Friday & kind offers of assistance, and on Saturday about 30 persons attended the funeral without invitation. Mr Hibberd made a beautiful address & prayer – he prayed for our "friends so far away" that when the sad intelligence should reach them they would be "comforted by the Giver of all consolation"; he accompanied us to the grave & committed all that was mortal of our precious jewel to the silent tomb. Our friends have been very kind & we feel that we have still many blessings left, but we long for the sympathy of those nearest & dearest to us. I hope you will excuse a short letter this time as I do not feel able to think on any other subject than our bereavement, not that I murmer at it – God has given us strength according to our day, & the grace of resignation to his will; we feel assured that "He hath done all things well". Our health is pretty good tho' dear John suffers much from headaches, & seems rather out of sorts, our rest has been so broken of late it is not at all surprising – dear Evelyn is cutting teeth which makes her very fretful: she also has a bad cold. We have been looking for letters from you for two or three weeks as we have not had any from Sheffield since Christmas Eve, and we begin to feel anxious about you. I hope we shall hear before we post these.

I remain

Your very affecte daughter

Mary H. Webb

P.S. Thursday Feby 11th 1858 Dear John is much better now & Evelyn has almost lost her cold: the former says I must tell you the seeds are for George. I wish you, dear Mother, or Susan would write a few lines to someone at Park Street & post at *one post* before the enclosed to Mother. I fear I have told her the sad tidings too abruptly, & it may be too great a shock for her.

Brother John would be the best person to tell her.

The weather has been very cold for three days – last night the thermometer was 13° below zero & the night before 14° degrees. In our parlor it was 11° above [sic] zero each morning before we made the fire. Our term is ended today. Adeline leaves us this week. Adieu excuse haste etc

Yours truly

M.H.W.

No 40 (39 is missing)

JSW

Dundee Kane Co Ill.

Augt 13th 1858

Very dear Parents,

You have learnt through Lizzie of our trip to Aurora & of my intention to visit the State of Iowa. On the monday after the date of my letter to her we received the welcome letters from Sheffield & Aughton together with a Yorkshire Gazette for which you have my thanks. Next day (2nd Aug^{t}) I started on my prospecting tour stopping at Dekalb, Polo, Dixon, & crossed the Mississippi on the morning of the 5th at Fulton. I then went on from Clinton on the west bank of the De Witt. Before I arrived there I heard that the late rains had made the road almost impassable, the river having flooded the road & made travelling by stage very uncertain. I therefore determined to relinquish my prescribed route & return by stage in a south easterly direction to the Mississippi to the city of Davenport. Long before I arrived there I was heartily glad that I had not proceeded. The stage left De Witt at 1 PM & after going three miles was stopped by the river Wapsipinicon which is usually fordable. There the passengers had to be conveyed upwards of two miles in a skiff, & a wagon at the opposite side took us forward. We did not reach Davenport till 7.30 though told it was only 12 miles from De Witt & had no covering from the roasting sun but our umbrellas. For this precious trip I paid $1½ or 6/2d sterling. From Davenport I came direct home on the 6th taking good observation of all the places we passed through & making enquiries when I could. Dear M.H. was much surprised at seeing me so soon, but when she had ascertained that there was nothing the matter she reconciled herself to my presence – even made a demonstration of pleasure. The country through which I passed was mostly what we call rolling prairie relieved here & there by woodland. Dixon is a beautiful little city of 5,000 inhabitants & contains a college. Polo has a population of about 1600, it is only three years old & supports two newspapers. It is a great grain depot for the country round. Davenport is the smartest city on my route. It contains from 15 to 20,000 &, rising gradually from the river exhibits its fine buildings to advantage. The night I was there a telegram had been received announcing the successful laying of the marine cable between

England & America, (*and* "Queen Victoria and the President of the U.S. had exchanged greetings through it." *according to the 1897 letters*) An impromptu meeting was called together by a band of music in front of the Post Office, & after the street multitude was called to order, a chairman was chosen & speeches delivered in honor of this great achievement of science. A committee was afterwards formed to procure an oration to be delivered at a future time in case the news proved true. A similar demonstration was I am informed made in every city & town on this continent. But you will be wondering whether I gained anything by my trip & whether I attained my object. My prospects were brightened by finding what I hope will prove a better location. Mr Clark, Congregational Minister at Dundee, had advised me to stop at Dekalb & referred me to Mr Bristol, a friend of his, in that place. I did so, & called on my arrival and he gave me the information I sought & the next morning called at my hotel & kindly spent some time in introducing me to some of the most influential people. I got there these particulars: Dekalb contains from 1000 to 2000 people, is scarcely 4 years old, is rapidly increasing contains three District Schools which are crowded to overflowing, no private schools but that the people feel very little interest in the subject of education. The last item caused many to discourage me from my idea of setting up an Academy & Mr Bristol himself was far from sanguine. As I proceeded on my journey I pondered the matter over until it became clear that I must search more closely into it. On Sunday (9th) M.H. & I & Eva went down and during the afternoon of that day & the next morning I saw about 25 of the heads of houses & got from them the promise of about 30 pupils. I thought *that* a sufficient ground of success & after putting an advertisement in the paper to the effect that I intended opening a school, we returned home on the 10th to mature & carry into effect our plans. This is our position & I trust we shall have your prayers & good wishes in our new enterprise. Mr & Mrs Bristol were very kind to us, we took tea with them on the monday & Mr B accompanied me to many of his friends and spoke for me as if I were his brother.

There is something so revolting in servitude to one who has tasted liberty that nothing but a strong sense of duty could induce me to be again enthralled. Mr Smith's service is altogether impossible for on joining the Sons of Temperance I pledged myself neither to make buy sell or use as a beverage any spirituous or malt liquor, wine or cider & I am so convinced of the evil arising from even a moderate use of the accursed thing that I look upon the trade with abhorrence. Dundee is rightly called a one horse town & can scarcely be said to increase as only six houses have been built since we came to it.

A few items of our cost of living may be interesting to you:

An easy way to get an approximate value of the above in sterling is to take half the number of cents for pence, this first total. 7.55½ cents is equal to 3.77¾ or 31/5¾ d. For the whole time to July 20 our expenses have averaged 26/- sterling per week including everything & deducting 2/10d. per week the cost of extra furniture our expenses have only been 23/2d. per week. We have not been extravagant, have we? M.H. did not make me a plum pudding on my birthday though she promised she would if I would get some currants but I was too idle to go to the store. We have no rhubarb in the garden.

I wish Lizzie was here, she would be invaluable as an assistant in my new school besides she might obtain a large music class.

Believe me to be as ever Your affectionate son John S. Webb.

No 36

JSW

Dekalb

Dekalb Co Ill.

Oct 18th/58

Very dear sister Susan,

Our letters will have been expected sometime but the delay will be explained & excused when you are informed of our being so fully occupied in preparing and fixing our new abode. We began to pack up our household stuff as early as 23rd Augt but not being able to make arrangements by letter to rent a building, I came down again to Dekalb on 31st Aug & the same day bought the building & lot & next day agreed to a contract for the addition to be builded to the schoolroom of which my purchase only consisted. For the said room (which was built four years ago by the Methodists for a meeting house) they asked a rent of $87 per annum & even at that rate we were liable to be turned out at any month's end. As there was no other room to be had suited to my purpose & as I should have had to lay out considerable money on the schoolroom even if I had rented it & moreover as they offered it for sale at a low price, I thought it would be the best way to make it my own. Another consideration was, that we could not get a house to live in at a less rent than $100 which with the school rent would be equal to £38 a year which would be a great lift out of our income. The accompanying plan will give you some idea of our establishment which we dignify with the name of Dekalb Academy.

The schoolroom will accommodate about 80 pupils. The school porch which is part of the addition is fitted with shelves & hooks for a cloakroom. On the front gable of main building I have had built a belfry & hung a bell of 60 lbs weight in it the first & only large bell in Dekalb. I am using my old Dundee desks which I planed & put together afresh & which look almost like new ones. Besides my old forms I have eight long seats with backs very useful for class purposes. There are others which belong to the house scattered about town which I hope to get. My rostrum is at the upper end of the room so that I can step on it from my study door. The stove is in the middle of the room & the pipe goes into the chimney which projects into the pantry. You will smile at the small dimensions of our dwelling, & the poetical idea of love in a cottage may occur to your mind. If so cherish it, for in our case it is no fiction. The plan of it is the joint production of dear M.H. & self, before we had determined on buying the property. Though so small it is very snug & convenient & amply sufficient for our accommodation. Though the ground is not damp, yet the ground being flat we found it impossible to make a dry cellar, & though we much regretted being without, we thought it better to have none than a wet one. We had a good cistern dug under the pantry, well bricked & plastered which supplies us with plenty of water. We depend on our neighbours for spring water, but this is no great matter as one pail full a day supplies our want. The sitting room stove pipe passes through the pantry wall into the chimney. There is also one entry from the study. The whole building is of wood as are all the buildings in Dekalb except one, & is only one storey high. To make the house warmer in winter & cooler in summer I had a coat of lath & plaster put on between the studs or uprights half way between the outside boards or sidings and the inner plaster walls, making as it were three distinct walls with two dead spaces. The pantry is well supplied with shelves and a little cupboard under the chimney. My old sea-chest occupies an honorable position as a bin for flour and mealbags

167

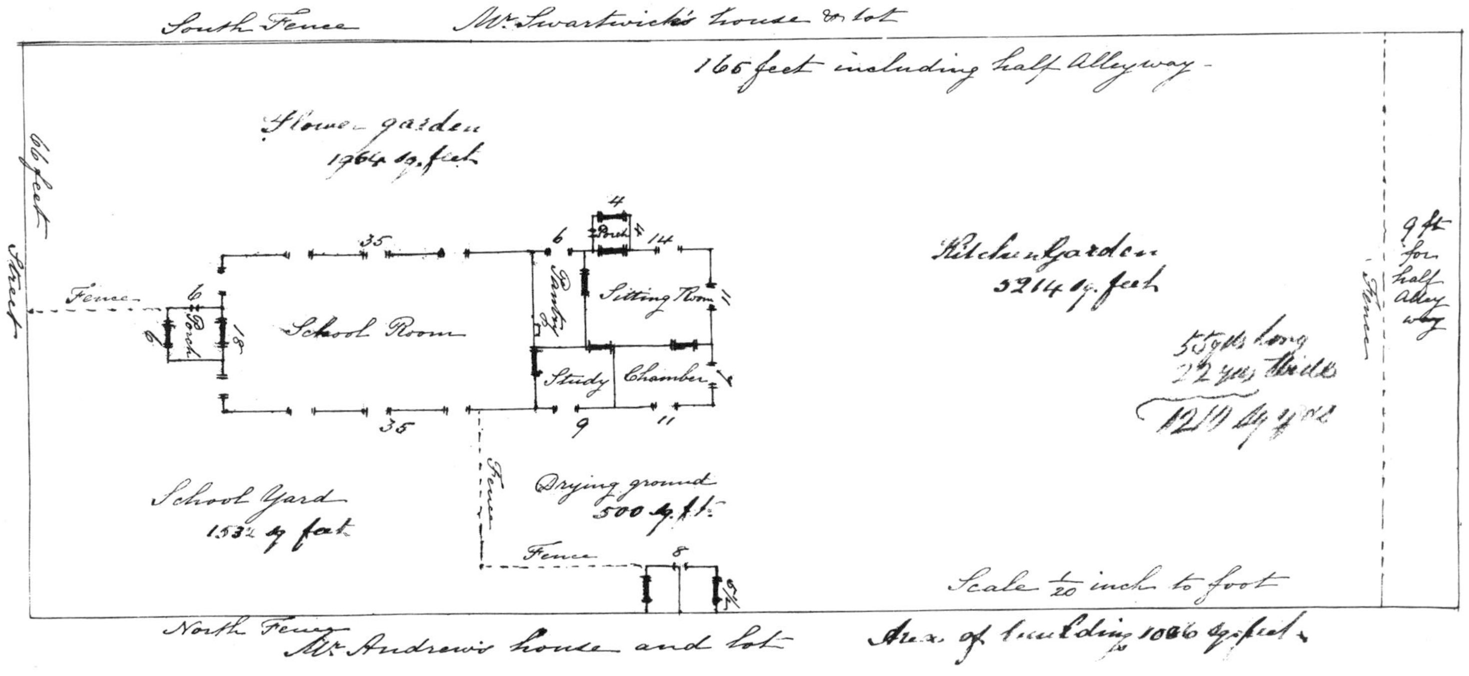

Plan of Dekalb schoolroom and gardens

etc. & the top of it for a dresser. Our library is in the study and in a conspicuous position hangs my father's black portrait & observations that have been made on his appearance would make his ears burn. Although the house & schoolyard occupy so much space I have yet 150 sq.ft. more for kitchen garden than I cultivated in Dundee besides 1964 sq.ft. for flowers & shrubs. (*from the 1897 letters*: "I had the land ploughed with bullocks, painting done, trees planted, a rostrum with a good plastered black board behind") the extra space available for planting is owing partly to the difference in the size of the lot that being only 60 x 150 and this 66 x 165 & to the quantity of grass. I kept there equal to 3276 sq.ft., a great part of which being the brow of a hill would have been too stoney for garden. Here are no stones. The soil is black loam with a subsoil of clay. To return to Dundee which I did on the 2nd Sept after making the necessary arrangements for the new house, I then set to work in good earnest to get in my garden stuff &c & my debts & packing up of goods. I had also a good deal of visiting to do. Our friends showed us much kindness & expressed so much regret that we felt very sorry to leave them. Having chartered a car at the depot in Dundee, Mr Marshall & I on the 15th Sept carted our stuff to it. The total charge all the way from Dundee to Dekalb 46 miles for the 4300 lb at 15c was only $6.45 or 26/6 sterling. Carting to the depot cost 6/- sterling. As I occupied the whole of a freight car they were not touched by any but myself & my helpers that I could take care that nothing was damaged. Everything came to hand safely, even the pickles were not spilled, and the crockery and glass all unbroken. We opened the boxes with hope & fear & were delighted & thankful with the result. Glass & crockery being imported from England, & transported 1000 miles before they reached our prairie State, the cost of them here bears no comparison to what you pay in Eng^{d}. We slept at Mr Young's the night we sent the furniture off & next day I bade adieu to Dundee. On arriving at Dekalb I found the building but little advanced. The frame only was up & half the roof on. I was glad that M.H. had remained with her numerous friends. She did not arrive till the 28th. In the meantime I was living at the hotel, spending each day at the building, directing everything, cleaning my stoves, planing my desks, & cutting cordwood ready for fuel. I helped to cart away my goods from the depot on the 20th & stored them in the schoolroom The sundays & most evenings I spent with our new & kind friends the Bristols. M.H. came on the 28th when the first coat of plaster was only just hard but the Bristols offered us a home till ours was ready. On the 30th the plastering being finished we commenced cleaning & unpacking & by afternoon got our stove up & our kettle boiling. We continued to sleep at Mr Bristol's until the 7th Octr. On the saturday previous at 3 o'clock the carpenters took away their bench from out of the schoolroom & I commenced the task of cleaning it. When I tell you that besides the floor being covered with wood & shavings, the whole of the plaster had been scraped off the side walls on it, to make way for new coat; it having been cracked in moving the building you will have some idea of the Stygean Stable. In three hours all was cleared away, & the floor swilled & mopped, but my bones ached all night so that I could not sleep. At 4 o'clock on monday morning M.H. & I got up & with Eva came down to the door to go home but the morning was so dark & stormy that I persuaded M.H. to stop & go to bed again while I putting my nightgown over my clothes sallied forth & groped my way in the darkness.

I was very busily occupied until 9 o'clock putting my desks together & fixing my schoolroom stove. All was ready at school time & I commenced my scholastic duties with 4 pupils. Two more came in the afternoon making only six for the first day. The 2nd day I had 11, the 3rd 14, the 4th 16, one of whom has not been since, the 6th 20, the 7th 21, the 8th 22, the 11th 25, today the 20th I had one addition but as one left on account of a bad cough I only had 25 pupils to this date. This is much less than I expected & less than Dekalb will supply me in better times, but the farmers have suffered so much from poor crops that many who are willing are not able to patronise a private school. I am sanguine of having as large a school as I can manage during the winter term.

Except five who are all tolerable readers the rest are mostly grown up from 16 to 20 years old. So far we have not much improved our condition as we should probably have had as good a school in Dundee this term. The advantage is prospective & consists in a large population & more convenient premises. You must not suppose that we have paid for our new property. As yet only a small portion is paid & we shall find very tight work to scrape the installments together as they come due, but by the blessing of God on diligent endeavours we hope to make it really our own. We consider our investment is worth 25 per cent to us at least & the saving of such a heavy rate is better than paying the same in rent. Besides this I am likely to make arrangements with the Congregationalists for the use of the room on sundays for service which will realise me a little rent. I suppose you will want to know something of Dekalb. By the bye tell father not to put an accent over the e. It is situated in the centre of Dekalb county on the Dixon Airline [sic] Railroad, 58 miles west of Chicago so that we are 10 miles further from that city than we were when in Dundee. It is the centre of a large trade principally in grain, $7,000,000 of which were exported fall of 1857; the receipts ranged as high as 30,000 bushels a day. (*From the 1897 letters*: Dekalb was larger than Dundee, more shops and more people with a good sized hotel. It was mostly level, had plankside walks, a little wood on one side which was shared by birds and squirrels, two churches same as in Dundee. We made many good friends in Dekalb first & foremost of whom were Mr Bristol and his wife.) The country surrounding is undulating and the soil very rich & productive. The western boundary is formed by a large grove, through which the Kishwaukee flows on its way to unite with Rock River. This is but a small stream compared to the noble Fox River just as the undulations look quite flat compared with its high bluffs. Sweet Dundee will live in our memories for ever. The railroad runs through the centre of the village. One street which extends north and south crosses it at right angles 160 yards or more below our house. Mr Bristol's house is on the opposite side of the same street about 200 yards above us. Opposite his house a space has been left for a public square east of which stands the Baptist Ch. On the next street still further east & nearer the railroad, is the Methodist Ch. Both these buildings are large, well pewed & finished & are entirely of wood except the foundation. Mr Moxson is the Bap. Min., a very pleasant man & good preacher, moreover an Englishman, a Cockney born & bred. He sends me an adopted daughter. Mr Brown is the Meth. Min. A very good preacher. We have not got acquainted yet as he does not live in town having been appointed at a late conference & not got his family removed here. The Congregationalists have not yet built a church & have met hitherto in the District School House on the opposite side of our street near the Railroad. There are Universalists also who meet in the large district school house in the north side of the village. Mr Roberts, the Episcopal minister of Sycamore, has occasionally held a service in the Baptist Ch.

My own school room was occupied by the Roman Catholics previous to my taking it & a confessional, altar, & reading desk had been temporarily fitted up for their use. Main street where all the stores are, runs near the north side of the railroad & at an acute angle to it. There is a bank, about 6 grocery stores, several dry goods stores, two tailors, 3 milliners, one hardware, two turners, two barbers, two drug stores, a harness stores, three shoemakers, several lawyer's offices, fruit stores, bakery, two hotels, painters, butchers, post office &c &c &c besides new stores that are being builded. Near the depot is a good clean grist mill & two large warehouses, several lumber yards &c. The population is nearly 2,000 probably.

. . . .

I did not tell you that we are still unpainted. When that is done & the walls papered, the fences put up & the gardens planted we shall have a little Eden.

Our united love to you all

I am as ever Your affec. brother John S. Webb

P.S. I threw away before leaving Dundee the two pair of square toed boots Witheford made for me 5½ years ago. They have been very serviceable in the country, though too unfashionable for New York City.

No 42
JSW

Dekalb

Dekalb Co Ill.

Nov 30 1858

Dear George, I sat down after supper this evening to write a long letter to you but various things have conspired to hinder me until I find it more than 8½ o'clock & in this primitive country where we breakfast at 7 & dine & 12 we do not usually exceed 9½ in retiring. I will however make a commencement. Imprimis. Many thanks for yours. . . . .

You speak of our land of peaches. I regret to say that tho' large crops of peaches have been raised in this part of Illinois yet the climate is too severe occasionally to make them a certain crop. Three winters ago the trees were nearly all killed down & peaches are consequently rare & dear.

In Egypt as the southern part of Illinois is often called they raise considerable [sic] but Pennsylvania & New Jersey grow the largest crops. By the Bye have you planted any young peach trees to take the place of the old ones? In America they begin to bear at three years old & are usually worn out in four years id est., at 7 years of age they are all standard trees with us.

Mother Church is very poorly represented in the West. We have no Epis[1] church here but there is a small one in Sycamore, the county town served by Mr Roberts. An episcopal clergyman, Todd by name, lives in Derwent, 11 miles west. He held a service in this Baptist church at which we attended & were much pleased to join again in the beautiful liturgy. He came down to Dekalb with a view of organising a church but met with so little encouragement that we have heard no more about it. After service Mr Todd & Mr Moxson, the Baptist minister, accompanied us home to supper. The latter is a very pleasant conversational man, 20 years out from England, & an estimable man & fluent preacher.

I am glad to hear of your good prospects & trust that you will realise all your hopes. As for the apple trees I envy you. Oh that we had such an orchard! My garden is yet in grass, but the spring will, I trust, find improvement & by hard labor we may make it all we desire. Your surprise at our scarcity of fruit is natural but we have had very poor harvests in Illinois both of grain & fruit, but the low price to which wheat has settled shows that considerable has been grown elsewhere. Apples are quite a rarity this year. Last year we bought them at 50c or 2/- sterling a bushel. The last time I asked the price of this year's they were 60 cents or 2/6 per peck.

. . . .

It was a great pity that you did not succeed in ripening tomatoes. If you prized & appreciated them as we do you would be at considerable trouble another year to perfect them. But until persons become acquainted with their peculiar flavour they do not like them. M.H. was sometime before she was initiated but now is very fond of them. I would advise you to grow them under glasses another year. They are very tender & are killed by the first frost. Please to say if you wish any more seed, if so I will send you some. I have an excellent kind of bean called Lima bean, smaller than the Windsor bean but of much finer flavour, & not so coarse. There is a further advantage that not only is it good gathered green & eaten as the Windsor bean but the seed when taken up may be kept all winter or longer & cooked when wanted. If you cannot get them in England I will send you one or two in a letter from which you can raise seed. It is a climber & grows like the scarlet runner but bears a white flower. We also grow dwarf beans which if gathered young are quite equal to the scarlet runner & requires no poles & if allowed to seed may be cooked the same as the Lima beans but are not so good.

I do not think we have ever told you how we can have sweet corn through the winter. We gather it when the corns are plump & well set but not hard, & boil it & then scrape or rather cut off the corn from the cob & dry it thoroughly in the sun. When wanted for use it is steeped overnight & boiled & served with melted butter sauce. The sweet corn is a variety of Indian Corn & may be known by the shriveled [sic] appearance of the seed while the common corn is round & plump & on a larger cob. We have got a famous bag of seeds to plant our new garden with, a large variety of flower seeds many of which were given us in Aurora. At present these beauties in embryo can flourish only in imagination. For three weeks the ground has been covered with snow, the first of which fell on Nov 12th – again on the 20th, 23rd, 27th, 28th. How much longer it will remain I don't know, but it seems early for winter to set in. We have not yet had any severe cold. I have kept account of the thermometer, which hangs up in our sitting room, every morning before lighting fire, from the 14th Nov^{r} & have found it to range from 26° to 45°. You will be pleased to learn that though disappointed somewhat in my expectations, I have made a tolerable commencement in my new undertaking. Since the 1st Novr we have numbered 30 & as this term will be out on the 17th inst. I do not expect more until the winter term begins which will follow on the 20th without any vacation. I have no idea what number I may then have, but live in hope or rather dependence on Him who has promised that our bread & water shall be sure. As I apprehended a lack of accommodation, I had on the 30th Octr two new desks made to seat 8 pupils. I have now desks for 38 & plenty of space to fit up more if wanted. Besides the forms to the desks I have nine long seats with backs which will hold more than 40 adults. I told Susan in my last letter that the Congregationalists wished to have my room for their services. On one sabbath only bible classes & sabbath school meet there, & on the alternate sabbath a regular service morning & afternoon in addition to these, is held by our pastor, Mr Bristol. On every Wednesday evening is a prayer meeting & every two months there is a church meeting preparatory to the communion the following sabbath. (Mr Bristol ministers to a church in Dement, a village eleven miles west on the alternative sabbath). My room was occupied by them for the first time on the 17 Oct[r]. A great work of grace has been going on in Dement special daily services have been held there for several weeks by our common pastor Mr B., assisted by Mr Baxter from St. Charles & many have been converted from sin or backsliding & the little church which was dropping & ready to despair has had its strength renewed like the eagle. In happy England where endowed churches are open to the poor without money or price you have no idea of the difficulties & struggles to maintain the preaching of God's word in our little Prairie villages & hamlets, or the heavy heart consequent on the forced relinquishment of the public ordinances, or the joy & gratitude which pervade the church of the few sheep in the wilderness when God has thus evidently appeared on their behalf. This state of things is owing chiefly to the fact that western pioneers are seldom large capitalists & are therefore obliged to sink their little "all" in land buildings & tools & trust to their harvest for food for their families & any trifle obtained over & above necessary supplies it is advisable to sink annually in improving their farms. Thus years elapse before anything can be spared for social or religious privileges, much less superfluities. The American Home Missionary Society has done much for the West by supplying or increasing stipends. The yearly income of our minister seldom exceeds $600 & often *very* much less.

Dear M.H. & I have joined the Congregational Church. We presented our letter from St. John's Ch in Eliz[th] City which was read on Nov[r] 7th AM after service and a vote having been unanimously passed for our reception, we thereby became full members. On the evening of the same day we had a very interesting concert of prayer for the Missions, at which several interesting addresses were given. It is to be held monthly. On the 6th I finished building a woodshed which had been commenced by one man the day before. It is a necessary adjunct in which to stow our winter fuel. It is a singular coincidence that exactly one year ago I was building the porch & closet to our Dundee home. On the 8th Mr Ingraham called on me to make arrangements for the use of my room for a singing school every monday evening. He commenced one the monday after that & not succeeding in obtaining a sufficient number he gave it up. On the 9th the painting of the outside of the building with one coat was finished, which is all I can afford at present. The inside is neither papered nor painted yet & must remain as it is for an indefinite time. Being completed & neatly furnished & the woodwork & plaster all new, it still looks very clean & comfortable. My front fence which is to be of pickets is not yet fixed up & unless the snow goes & gives place to moderate weather, it can not be put up till spring. The 11th Novr was a day to be remembered on account of my promotion to the rank of one of the sovereign people. I went down to Geneva by the noon train & took out my second papers on final certificate as a citizen of the United States. This was expedient on becoming a property owner as no alien can legally bequeath real estate. It also gives me the opportunity of adding my vote in behalf of the principles of religious freedom & temperance & as the ballot box governs the councils of the nation so every single vote has influence for good or evil. Even if the better influence is in the minority it will be respected according to its numerical strength. On the 12th we commenced burning coal in the school room & I anticipate much trouble in consequence as the coal soon fills up the pipes with soot. I have fired it once & cleared it out twice already. Coal is found in immense quantity in nearly all parts of the States. As there are no mines in our neighbourhood, it is expensive costing $5 or 20/8 sterling per ton of 2000 lb. The lead mines in Galena & in the neighbouring State of Wisconsin are among the richest in the world. Salt springs are also found.

Decr 6th '58

We have attended one of the Ch. Society Meetings. They are not so numerously attended as in Dundee. Mr Moxson had a donation visit on Novr 19th at which he received about sixty dollars. On the 20th M.H. put up Eva's hair in paper & on the next day (sunday) she appeared in curls for the first time. She looks quite cunning.

On the 24th I recd three Telegraph papers from Sheffield. My dear father has my best thanks for the same. The 25th was our annual Thanksgiving Day. School was closed. I attended the Baptist Ch. in the morning & walked out to make a call with M.H. in the afternoon. The Methodists had a supper at the hotel on the occasion at which they raised by the sale of tickets about sixty dollars towards purchasing new lamps for the church. The 29th was a great day to us for we received letters from Sheff^d & Manch^r. We longed as we read them together at night to be amongst you & almost regretted our decision, but we thought of the decided manner in which our duty had been pointed out & contented ourselves in the fulfillment of God's will. If He sees good we shall yet be permitted to see you again & our satisfaction will then be greater than if we were to follow only our own perverse inclinations. I attended on the 3rd inst. the meeting of the Literary Society which has recently been established here. The question discussed was "Ought capital punishment to be abolished". It fell to my lot to speak in the negative though much against my own convictions.

The monthly church meeting took place on saturday afternoon. After the usual religious exercises some business was attended to, the most important item of which was to re-engage Mr Bristol as pastor for another year & if possible to obtain sufficient subscriptions to keep him altogether & have services every sabbath. It was delightful to see the unity & readiness to sacrifice on the part of all. Yesterday we partook of the communion & also entered into covenant with the church according to their prescribed practice. But my paper is expended & though I should like to go on a little longer I must conclude. With love to you all, I am as ever,

Your affec. brother John S. Webb

No 41
JSW

Dekalb
Dekalb Co Ill.
March 24th/59

Mr & Mrs Webb
My very dear Parents,

It was with great pleasure that we rec^d & read last evening the budget from Sheffield & Manchester containing no less than sixteen letters. How could we think ourselves neglected or forgotten with such an accumulation of loving words as they contained.

. . . .

But in your own case you may be ready to conclude that like the unfortunate marine cable connexion must be imperfect or I should not now have so many as eight letters to answer in one telegram. I have just been reading them all over but do not find anything which requires any comment except father's suggestion respecting my carrying on a little trade in Sheff^d & Birm^m goods. The fact is, not that I despise or dislike either trade or the profit arising therefrom, but the people are so short of money that they now buy only necessaries. To say that they are poor would not describe their condition for they possess property but cannot realise cash.

You caution us against the wolves & bears. There was an account of a bear being killed near the town lately in the Dekalb paper but I cannot vouch for the truth as I made no enquiries about it. You are mistaken in saying that we do not enjoy the fruits of our garden. We reaped one year's crop from that in Eliz^th City & two years from the one in Dundee. The 9th & 10th were awfully cold days.

On the 11th a sad affliction befell our dear pastor. He had been chopping some wood for fuel & as he was about to enter his house he picked up a stick & tapped one end on the ground to shake off the snow. It hit a small chip which it tripped with violence against his left eye. The result has been the temporary if not total loss of sight. The sight of the right eye was destroyed some years ago by an accident. Dear Mr B still entertains hope that his sight may be restored but the physician says that though possible it is not probable. The inflammation has not yet subsided. He bears this dreadful bereavement with most exemplary christian resignation. He is indeed a pattern to his flock. His dear wife also bears up well under the trying circumstances which weigh in a peculiar manner upon her. On the 13th Feb we held a special service in the morning for the sabbath schoolchildren, brothers Newitt, Wood & myself addressed them. Their number is much increased since they commenced meeting in my school room. They were so few at that time that some of the teachers had serious thoughts of giving it up altogether, but were induced to make an effort the result of which has been most gratifying. On the evening of the same day we had a concert of prayer on behalf of this interesting branch of our church. Dear M.H. was suffering at this time from a gathered breast, but the plaster from Manchester soon brought it to a head, & it discharged on the 15th Feb. I am thankful to say that she has had no further trouble with it. We rec^d same day a Yorkshire Gazette. We rec^d an Elgin paper publishing the sad defection of our late pastor Mr Hibbard of Dundee to the Universalists. He is a talented & promising young man, & was much esteemed by his flock, who were much grieved & shocked by the change in his sentiments. In a letter we rec^d from a friend Miss McClure, an active & zealous member of the church, we learnt that the change in his views has been going on for six months, & that during that time he has been taking Universalist papers. I suppose you know what that deadly heresay is. It is subversive of the fundamental principles of christianity; viz. human depravity, & the sacrificial atonement, it ignores the personality of Satan, the existence of hell the justice & truth of God. It asserts the ability of man to advance himself in holiness by his own unaided efforts. It deifies man & materializes God.

The Leeds Intelligencer arrived on the 26th Feb. On the 27th the Rev^d Mr Buss who took Mr Bristol's late charge in Dement preached three times. On the 3rd baby * was taken very sick & on the 4th I was obliged to call in Dr Smith to her. For some days we suffered much anxiety on her account & poor Eva had also a boil in her ear which made her cry night & day. I am thankful to say that both are now well. On March 6th our dear pastor met with us for the first time since his accident. He did not hold a regular service, but what is called a church meeting. It was an affecting sight to see him enter the room with his face bound up. Many were the tears shed & when he spoke to us there was not a dry eye in the house. M.H. was not in the room but had the two doors open & could therefore hear all that was said.

The 8th was the last day of the winter term, we closed it in the afternoon by the reading of our Manuscript by the editors Hatty Tappen & I.V.Hiland, some class exercises in spelling, concert reading, & mental arithmetic & declamations. Quite a number of visitors were present. On the 9th I finished papering our sitting room which now looks very snug though as yet no painting has been done. I recommenced school on the 14th with only five pupils. This is the last day of my second week & I have only seven. This is a severe disappointment & owing to the times I have little hope of any great improvement until after harvest. Mr Buss again held services on the 13th & the 20th. Mr Bristol was sufficiently recovered to fulfill his duties amongst us. He preached two excellent services on that day.

---

* born 5.1.'59 & named Lucy Dora, my grandmother,TB.D.

Yesterday a man was putting down my front picket fence & soon as the ground is dry enough I shall have my lot plowed [sic] & try to fix, no not *fix*, to make my garden. Do not be anxious about us, if teaching does not succeed, I shall try something else.

With love, Yrs John S. Webb

one of Eva's latest: Ma, where do you get the milk from that is fast to you? Did you buy it & put it in?

another: Ma, what do you want both chil'n for?

MHW

Dekalb Ill

Augst 26th/59

Mr & Mrs Webb,

My very dear Parents,

I suppose you are now settled in your 'new' house. I hope you find it more convenient than the old one. It seems very long since we heard from you, your last letters were received the last saturday in June, we are looking anxiously for a budget from Sheffield every day. Our letters from Manchester this week contain the sad intelligence of dear John J. Glover. It is a sad bereavement to my dear Lizzie. They were hoping to be married in October. Truly God's way is "mysterious" & "past finding out" but we know that "all things work together for good to them that love Him".

We had a very busy time this week for yesterday we entertained the Ladies' sewing circle connected with our Church: they meet every fortnight & each person pays a fee (5c) the funds are devoted to the Church or Sunday school: we had tea in our school room; 27 in all.

What will Grandpapa say when I tell him that last Tuesday dear John killed a snake in our garden! It measured 19 (not feet) inches! We have had a very dry summer, scarcely any rain, I don't think we have had more than two wet days in the last three months. The potatoes have suffered much: their tops are literally burnt off, & the tubers very small. The harvest is all over except corn & the crops *good*, but very thin. We have already made bread of the new flour & it is excellent: we are enjoying the luxuries of green corn & tomatoes, the latter have only just begun to ripen. Soon after we sent off our last letters baby cut 2 teeth and she seems to be about getting more, for she is cross & not well.

I finished my school duties a fortnight yesterday & was not at all sorry to do so. I think dear John has a better prospect of getting a school than he has had for some time: he intends commencing next Monday but one.

You will be glad to learn that I have some help with my work now. We have had a very nice girl living with us the last fortnight – her name is Anna Roberts, she is seventeen, rather tall & pretty & able to do all kinds of work, and also *very willing*: she takes the washing & ironing off my hands and helps me considerably besides – she goes in school during lesson time & I have not to pay her for her services as board is considered sufficient compensation. She is an English girl from Chester, has been in the country about nine years, has lost both her parents & been adopted by a family who have lived here this summer but have now left – confided her to us for the winter in order that she may have the benefit of education; I think we shall like her very much: I am quite in arrears with my sewing as I have scarcely done any since Dora was born, and both the children grow fast. I have also to make preparations for winter. We have had a good deal of cold weather already, but yesterday was quite warm, & today we cannot bear the windows and doors shut: we have had no rain this summer or autumn, & water is very scarce, the wells are almost all dried & if we do not have rain soon we shall suffer much: we had a good supply of rainwater from our own cistern, but many of our neighbours have had none for a long time.

We are very much interested in the accounts of the Great Eastern but are almost out of patience at its many delays.

Accept our united best love & give a portion to all your circle, also to dear George & Sarah & the children and

believe me ever

Your very affect^e daughter
Mary H. Webb

No 42
JSW

Dekalb
Dekalb Co Ill
Novr 2nd/1859

Dear Parents,

We delayed our answer to your last budget till we should receive letters from Manchester.

We are all well, thank God, & prospering as well as we can expect in such hard times. We have thirty-one pupils in attendance but only 20 part of this term. Three weeks is all that is now unexpired. My school is a very interesting one – 17 of my pupils are nearly grown up, some taller & stouter than me, 10 of the rest are tolerable readers & 4 are primary scholars which last are kindly taken off my hands by dear M.H. I open school every morning at 9, by reading of scriptures & prayer & sometimes the children sing one of the pretty hymns which they learned in the sabbath school. We are all very happy together, cherishing kindly feelings, keeping good order & discarding all punishments. Occasionally the pupils write compositions which are read by two of themselves appointed as editors. I feel more at home in the school room than the counting house, but I have such an increasing conviction of the responsibility resting on the teacher of youth that with my limited capabilities I shrink from it & intend on returning to England to obtain some mercantile employment if possible.

(Nov 5) The ordinary routine of events has been invaded of late by various disturbing causes. Three weeks ago we had a pleasant visit from Mrs Goodwin wife of Dr Goodwin of Dundee who with her son, drove over & stopped with us one day & night. Fred^{k} her son, was one of my pupils & is much attached to me. On the friday evening of the same week the children of the sabbath school had a grand time at the Methodist Ch. The teachers & friends had intended having a picnic in the grove some time ago, but the cold weather came on suddenly & prevented it. The exercises of the evening consisted of singing & declamations by the children & addresses, also in the distribution of cake & apples & candy. They sang beautifully some appropriate songs such as "I have a father in the promised land", "We all love one another" &c. The following week the teachers of Dekalb Co held an Institute, the particulars of which you could read in Sycamore Sentinel. We have no newspaper published in Dekalb. On the tuesday afternoon I closed school at 3 PM & with my senior pupils went to the Institute. Feeling interested in it I determined to adjourn my school until the following monday & take an active part in its exercises. I also assisted the commissioner in examining the teachers in grammar & arithmetic. Four of my pupils were candidates & attained their certificates. The week after, Professor Suffern held a musical convention. The best singers in the neighbourhood met together morning, afternoon & evening every day during the week for rehearsal & on the saturday evening gave a concert. M.H. & I went to the latter & were much pleased. There is a growing interest in music & much improvement is evident during the past year.

Our sabbath school flourishes. Some time ago we formed a Sabbath School Association to meet monthly, each member to pay 25c. entrance fee & 5c per month. Singing, addresses & social conversation occupy the two hours we spend together. We have only had three meetings & have already raised eight dollars with which to increase the S.S. "Library". Last thursday the meeting numbered 65.

Crops (garden) have been poor, but are a considerable help to us. Amongst other things which our garden has produced have been a spontaneous crop of mushrooms. Last night I opened my schoolroom to a blind young lady who gave a concert & read out of a New Testament & also wrote. A collection was made for her at the close which realised only $3.10. We have apples cheaper than you. I had a box containing near 3 bushels from Chicago for which I paid $2.06 or 9d sterling a peck.

From your loving son

John S. Webb

No 38 S

JSW

Dear Sister Susan,

I sat down this evening purposely to write to you but much of the time has been occupied 'making a trade' with a neighbour for some cord wood in exchange for a comfortable or bedspread [sic] & an ewer & bason [sic] Rather ominous you may think, John must be either short of money, or he is preparing to return. You are right both ways, but you must not suppose that we are coming right off hand. This can not be as our current term only commenced on the 29th ult. The previous term expired on the 22nd & so many of my pupils were leaving that I had little reason to expect such a number in the winter term as would remunerate me. After much & prayerful consideration we determined on the alternative of continuing the school or selling all off & returning home. If we could obtain thirty pupils we decided that it would be better to stay through the winter. During the five days holiday we were in a very unsettled state. There seemed to be no prospect for a good school & I employed much of the time in seeking out purchasers for our furniture &c as it was important to lose no time lest we might have to travel in the depths of winter. Up to monday noon my list of names was several short of the required number. Several of the youths who were anxious to attend were exerting themselves to obtain more. We were already calculating whether it would be possible to be with you on Christmas Day or New Years's. The ringing of the bell next morning at 9 o'clock was to be the signal for the school to assemble but the time was passing away & all expectation of success was at an end. Will you believe that when towards evening & early next morning more than the required number was obtained that a feeling of disappointment came over me & I opened school with more resignation than pleasure. I know it is better for us to remain here till spring, for travelling a thousand miles across the country at this time of the year would have exposed us to much inconvenience. We intend this to be the last term & as it will take us five or six weeks at least to sell off & collect our debts in, & as the weather will be growing more pleasant the longer we tarry, we shall not be likely to be home before May day. May God grant us a happy meeting. We anticipate it much – though whether we shall be able to submit to all the conventionalisms remains to be proved. When we think of the distance & of the expense it seems to be a terrible undertaking, but when we think that in two weeks we might accomplish it, the short time seems to diminish the difficulties. If as M.H. remarks we could only remove ourselves, house, fixings & all, it would be very nice for we are very comfortably settled. It seems such a pity after being at so much trouble & expense to leave our little home after so short an enjoyment of it. We are satisfied however, that as I have to begin life anew the sooner I start the better. And the prospect of meeting our dear relatives again gives us such exquisite pleasure as to counterbalance regrets for the past & misgivings for the future. But it is bedtime. Goodnight.

Decr 23rd. We have longer days here than you have. It was light till 5½ hours this evening. We are intending to visit Dundee on saturday & spend our Xmas holiday there. Our school will be closed one week. We now number *forty* pupils, the largest number I have ever had. Of these M.H. takes seven entirely off my hands and two more partially. My desks are nearly full though they are made to accommodate 38. Many of my pupils are larger than me & take up a deal of space. We propose at the end of the term to have an Exhibition similar to the one at Dundee & then – & then – Oh I begin to feel impatient at the thought – then – we shall prepare to take our departure from the Great West, to revisit our own, our native land, and enjoy again the presence of the dear ones at home. This term will be out at the end of the third week in Feb^y, but as I mentioned in our last letters, the closing of our affairs will take much time & we shall not hurry to come before the cold weather is gone. May God grant us a happy meeting! We have already had some severe weather. The ground is covered with snow & sleighs have taken the place of wheeled carriages. Winter is an expensive season – we have need of a large school. Cordwood at $4.50 per cord of 128 cubic feet & anthracite coal at $9.50 per ton of 2000 rapidly disappear. Water is very scarce as very little rain fell before the frost & snow came. For some weeks we have used no other than cistern water, of which we have had a continual supply. Others are not so fortunate & have had to fetch it a great distance.

What is to be my lot is hidden in the future, but I am satisfied that

He whose I am & whom I serve will redeem his word that my bread & my water shall be sure.

Give my hearty love to all

Goodnight. I am as ever

Your affect[e] brother

John S. Webb

Index of places mentioned